T0209196

Sales
Express

Leo Gough

- Fast-track **introduction to the sales process. Focuses on personal** selling, **effective sales management, key sales skills, and the** relationship **between sales and marketing**

- Covers the **latest techniques in CRM, key account management,** SPIN selling, **and relationship selling. Also deals with how to** improve key selling skills **such as prospecting, identifying** qualified **prospects, and the art of the close**

- Case studies from Dyson, Amway, the Japanese car market, and Sotheby's

- Includes a comprehensive resources guide, **key concepts** and thinkers, a 10-step **action plan, and a section of FAQs**

SALES

12.01

Copyright © Capstone Publishing, 2003

The right of Leo Gough to be identified as the author of this book has been asserted in accordance with the Copyright, Designs and Patents Act 1988

First Published 2003 by
Capstone Publishing Limited (a Wiley company)
8 Newtec Place
Magdalen Road
Oxford OX4 1RE
United Kingdom
http://www.capstoneideas.com

CIP catalogue records for this book are available from the British Library and the US Library of Congress

ISBN 1-84112-454-0

Wiley also publishes its books in a variety of electronic formats. Some content that appears in print may not be available in electronic books.

Websites often change their contents and addresses; details of sites listed in this book were accurate at the time of writing, but may change.

Substantial discounts on bulk quantities of Capstone Books are available to corporations, professional associations and other organizations. For details telephone Capstone Publishing on (+44-1865-798623), fax (+44-1865-240941) or email (info@wiley-capstone.co.uk).

Contents

Introduction to ExpressExec

ExpressExec is a completely up-to-date resource of current business practice, accessible in a number of ways – anytime, anyplace, anywhere. ExpressExec combines best practice cases, key ideas, action points, glossaries, further reading, and resources.

Each module contains 10 individual titles that cover all the key aspects of global business practice. Written by leading experts in their field, the knowledge imparted provides executives with the tools and skills to increase their personal and business effectiveness, benefiting both employee and employer.

ExpressExec is available in a number of formats:

» **Print** – 120 titles available through retailers or printed on demand using any combination of the 1200 chapters available.
» **E-Books** – e-books can be individually downloaded from Express-Exec.com or online retailers onto PCs, handheld computers, and e-readers.
» **Online** – http://www.expressexec.wiley.com/ provides fully searchable access to the complete ExpressExec resource via the Internet – a cost-effective online tool to increase business expertise across a whole organization.

» **ExpressExec Performance Support Solution (EEPSS)** – a software solution that integrates ExpressExec content with interactive tools to provide organizations with a complete internal management development solution.

» **ExpressExec Rights and Syndication** – ExpressExec content can be licensed for translation or display within intranets or on Internet sites.

To find out more visit www.ExpressExec.com or contact elound@wiley-capstone.co.uk.

Introduction

An introduction to "the highest-paid hard work and the lowest-paid easy work you can find."

In 1902 a 14-year-old immigrant arrived in New York, unable to speak a word of English. Getting a job writing prices on a blackboard in the New York Stock Exchange, this young immigrant, H.W. Dubiski, became enthralled by the novel concepts of sales training and sales management. Applying them to stock broking, Dubiski developed prepared speeches for his salesmen to use and held inspirational rallies. Every day the sales force would meet in the morning to sing, chant, and cheer, working themselves up into a frenzy of excitement before being sent out to sell stocks and bonds to the world. Dubiski built up his brokerage fast and sold it in 1914 for $5 million. He was only 26.

Inspirational stories of this kind are what every salesperson needs to keep on going in a world of indifferent customers, frosty personal assistants, and intense competition. It helps if the stories are true (as this one is). Europeans may laugh at American optimism and near-worship of the sales process, but many of the methods developed in the United States have proved effective, with some adaptation, in markets as diverse as Britain and Mongolia. The fact is that sales training works.

All businesses depend upon sales to survive, but personal selling is costly. Today, businesses have other, cheaper methods to achieve sales, such as call centres and Websites, that can handle repeat business efficiently. Personal sellers are the thoroughbreds of the selling business and have to be used effectively, so today they are generally found in specialized areas working in teams to make complex sales to multi-nationals, or calling on professionals such as doctors and architects as "missionaries" to persuade them to adopt their products.

Selling has become professionalized. The days of the door-to-door encyclopedia salesman are long gone, and salespeople are expected to have extensive knowledge of their products and a wide range of business processes. Regulation and customer sophistication have improved the ethics of selling, or at least devolved ethical questions to the higher reaches of a corporation. Many salespeople now have university degrees and considerable expertise in fields such as science, medicine, and engineering. The top performers continue to take the development of selling skills seriously and constantly work to extend their range of abilities – if you don't strive to improve, the chances are that you'll start to get worse. At best, sales can provide an enjoyable and financially rewarding career for a whole lifetime, although the chances are that you will move from one product group to another as markets change and new opportunities appear.

This title is an introduction to the selling field, which is extraordinarily diverse. Other ExpressExec titles in this module cover key aspects in more detail – the purpose here is to provide an overview of what has been called "the highest-paid hard work and the lowest-paid easy work you can find." Top salespeople continue to earn astonishing amounts in commission, and some of them subsequently become successful entrepreneurs and CEOs. They are worth it too – a sales champion generates the turnover that feeds everyone else in the business. Perhaps you will become one of them.

What is Sales?

- » Types of selling
- » Selling skills
- » How selling relates to marketing
- » Strategic marketing objectives
- » Sales management
- » The essentials of personal selling.

TYPES OF SELLING

In theory, every contact between a company and its customer is an opportunity to sell. Broadly, selling can be broken down into three distinct types:

» Creating orders
» Getting orders
» Taking orders.

Order creating – in complex industries, salespeople can influence sales by persuading individuals to recommend or specify their products to the actual customer. For instance, drug companies use "missionary" sales-people to encourage doctors to prescribe their proprietary medicines to patients, and producers of construction materials visit architects to persuade them to incorporate their products into the specifications for a building. Neither doctors nor architects are customers, but their support for a product has a direct influence on sales.

Order getting is the best-known sales function. It includes front line salespeople, such as the sales force that seek new prospective customers, sales teams who work on developing long-term relationships with large organizations, and salespeople who sell high-cost products such as insurance direct to consumers. Order getters are often supported by technical specialists or merchandisers who advise on store displays, organize in-store promotions, and keep tabs on stock levels.

Order taking relates to existing customers – a delivery, for instance, is an opportunity to ask the customers if they would like to restock other items that have sold, to inform them about new product lines, and to obtain information about their requirements. Sales success depends heavily on the reliability of the delivery service. "Inside" order takers work at the company's premises, for example as store assistants or telesales staff.

SELLING SKILLS

Fulfilling customers' needs is the essence of any business, but a sales-person's powers of persuasion are often a decisive factor in achieving a sale. Most products and services are not superior to the competition on all points, and traditionally a key element in the selling process is to emphasize the best features and benefits of a product. With the advent of relationship selling and global account management, where a supplier deals with many employees of one large customer, the focus is on nursing sales through many different individuals and committees, and the sales force tend to work much more closely as a team – closing a sale may take many calls, justified by the large size of the order.

Since repeat business is essential in most businesses, a deceptive, fast-talking approach is usually counter-productive – ultimately, companies employing the hard-sell and trickery are likely to lose out to less ruthlessly aggressive competitors.

HOW SELLING RELATES TO MARKETING

The concept of marketing developed in the United States in the 1950s out of a dissatisfaction with existing sales approaches. The core of the marketing philosophy is that the customer's needs are paramount; a business should identify customer needs and wants and then fulfil them, rather than insensitively imposing existing products and services upon the market. Marketing attempts a scientific approach: carefully analyzing the market and categorizing it into segments with definable needs and wants, finding unserved market gaps, designing products and promotional efforts to fit particular segments, and lastly targeting segments with the most potential for profit.

Central to any company's marketing efforts is the "marketing mix" – controlling the variables of pricing, product, promotion, and distribution to achieve the desired objectives.

Selling is, or should be, an integral part of marketing, but in many companies the two functions are often at odds. Salespeople, as front line troops, often resent what they perceive as arbitrary decisions made by the marketing department that damage their sales efforts. The point is that need for coordination derives from marketing planners, who have an overview.

STRATEGIC MARKETING OBJECTIVES

Many products have a lifecycle, and strategy alters according to the stage that the product has reached. Table 2.1 is an idealized model of how strategies may change over time.

Table 2.1

Market objective	Sales goal	Sales strategy
Build	Increase volume	High call rate on existing customers
Increase distribution	High focus during call	
Good service	Prospecting	
Hold	Maintain volume	Maintain call rates
	Maintain distribution	Medium focus
	Maintain level of call on new outlets when they appear	Service
Harvest	Reduce selling costs	Only call on profitable accounts
	Target profitable accounts	Other methods – telemarket or drop
	Reduce service costs and inventory	No prospecting
Divest	Clear inventory	Quantity discounts to certain accounts

SALES MANAGEMENT

As selling has become more professionalized, the role of the sales manager has broadened. Sales managers are no longer expected merely to be charismatic personalities who goad the sales force into achieving the target volume; they are now expected to play a key part in developing strategy, forecasting, and planning. Today's manager has a very wide range of skills, with primary responsibility for:

» Recruiting and training the sales force
» Deciding on the size of the sales force and allocating territories
» Setting sales objectives
» Motivation
» Forecasts and budgets
» Evaluating and controlling individual salespeople.

Sales managers are expected to have a thorough knowledge of marketing and to be able to work closely with the marketing department. Not all salespeople want to become sales managers – some top performers enjoy life in the field, and find that they can earn more by continuing to be "lone wolves." A sales manager is like the coach of a sports team – he or she may not have been the greatest performer on the road, but is talented at motivating and guiding others.

THE ESSENTIALS OF PERSONAL SELLING

Most successful salespeople emphasize the long-established basic model for making a sale, and argue that it is not possible to achieve consistent results without mastering all the skills the model describes, as follows.

Prospecting

Prospecting simply means the search for new potential customers, particularly by making personal calls, but also through enquiries generated from trade fairs and advertising. It is more often used in business-to-business selling than in business-to-consumer selling because professional customers are more easily accessible and the average sale tends to be higher, thus justifying the time and expense of prospecting.

While good sales organizations generally have formal systems for prospecting, top salespeople tend to put aside time for additional prospecting on their own. As sales guru Tom Hopkins puts it, "the way to make more money is to see more people." Regular prospecting is a good habit that many salespeople fail to develop because of the inevitability of a high rejection rate. Although it is much more comfortable to call on existing customers and old contacts, sales growth, particularly for products with a long life, depends upon constantly finding new customers.

Prospects can be graded for quality; the best ones are generally "referrals," meaning contacts who have been recommended by satisfied customers. The key here is that the customer must be enthusiastic about the product and have a liking for the salesperson, so that the referrals are to people who are genuinely likely to need the product. The referring customer often has detailed knowledge of their circumstances, which they can pass on to the salesperson.

Identifying "qualifying" customers

Someone who does not drive is unlikely to buy a car; an employee in a firm who does not have the authority to make a purchase will not do so. Salespeople spend an enormous amount of time talking to people who are not "qualifying" prospects; in other words, they will not buy because they either are unable to do so or have no need of the product. A major skill in selling is to prescreen prospects before visiting them to identify those who are likely to want the product. Three fruitful methods are:

» Referrals – a satisfied customer provides accurate information about a prospect's needs.
» "Orphans" – most companies have a high turnover of sales staff who leave a substantial number of buyers or near-buyers behind them. Much of the selling work has already been done, and many "orphans" are in the market for upgrades or new products.
» Exchanging leads – sales managers can be contacted in several firms that sell non-competing products to the same type of customer as you do and regular group meetings suggested to exchange information about potential customers. This is a powerful method that is mutually beneficial, but depends upon only allowing strong, motivated salespeople to attend.

Handling objections

Customers usually raise negative points during the selling process, if only to play devil's advocate, and much training is devoted to showing how salespeople can turn these "objections" to their advantage. Many objections can usefully be seen as a disguised request for more information about the product, while others may simply be a way of playing for time. Strong salespeople are quick to recognize objections that are insurmountable, such as the fact that the buyer does not have the money and cannot borrow it. Insurmountable objections are sometimes known as "conditions"; if they arise, the salesperson should simply disconnect from the selling process as courteously as possible.

Objections must be heard out – a salesperson who interrupts or "jumps" too hard on an objection is likely to alienate the customer. One effective technique is to listen carefully and then feed the objection back calmly. This sometimes has the effect of eliciting an answer to the objection from the customer, especially when two are present. Then you can ask the customer to elaborate in more detail, giving you time to compose the best answer. Many objections arise frequently, so salespeople who know their products have a range of satisfactory answers they can give. By studying the weak points of the product, no objection should come as a surprise, and in some cases a simple admission that the customer is right can result in a sale. Once the objection has been fully discussed, "confirm" that the customer has understood the answers and move on to the next topic.

Closing

In sales training, the most emphasized aspect of the selling process is how best to "close" a sale. A "close" occurs when the customer agrees to make the purchase, either by making a payment or by signing a binding agreement. A "close" can happen at any point in a presentation, and salespeople must be alert to the signs that the customer has come to a decision. Some key points to remember are:

» Try always to have prices at your finger tips – never pause to calculate taxes, freight costs, and the like. Any delay can ruin the "close." If you have to do sums, use a calculator – it looks more professional.
» Curb the urge to finish your prepared presentation. If the customer indicates the wish to buy, stop talking about the product and start filling in the order form.
» Get the order form out of your case early, so as not to frighten the customer off the purchase by making a big show of finding the papers.

"Trial closes" are attempts to see if the customer is ready to buy; typically they involve asking the customer details about the still hypothetical order, such as "Would you like it in blue?" or "Which delivery date is best for you, the 15th or the 30th?" Fill in the customer's answer on the order form, saying "I'll make a note of that." It is common to make four or five trial "closes" during a presentation before making the sale.

If a trial "close" works, move on to the actual "close." Experience shows that direct questions such as "Do you want to buy one?" often ruin the sale; the key at this delicate stage is to make the transition from presentation to decision as smoothly as possible. Salespeople are encouraged not to change their tone of voice or do anything to change the buyers' mood, such as asking them to go somewhere else to fill in the form. Often, buyers will not overtly express the wish to buy – but do not object as you fill in the order form and hand it to them to sign. On other occasions, you can obtain a sale by asking a question such as "Would you like it delivered next week?" followed by a long pause that forces the customer to make a decision.

There are a large number of closing tactics; see Chapter 8, "Closing techniques," for more details.

KEY LEARNING POINTS

» Salespeople can be divided into three main types: order getters, who make the sale; order creators, the "missionaries" who promote the product; and order takers, who deal with repeat orders from existing customers. Each job involves selling skills, but many people find that they are more talented at one role than the others.

» Marketing is, or should be, a rational strategic approach to maximizing sales of a product group over its natural lifecycle. Ideally the sales and marketing departments should coordinate closely, but this depends on good managers who understand the needs of their colleagues. Friction between sales and marketing people is usually a sign of poor management.

» The traditional model of personal selling is:

» Find prospects.

» Qualify them (make sure they might need the product and can pay for it).

» At presentations, listen to objections carefully before turning them into stated needs that your product can fulfill. Learn to spot unbeatable objections.

» When the signals are right, attempt "trial closes." The successful "trial close" becomes the actual "close."

Evolution of Sales

If sales skills are viewed as being primarily applied psychology, then there is a sense in which selling has had no evolution at all – the ability to persuade someone else that they need an object you are offering is as arguably as old as the human race itself. Retailing, in the form of a simple stall or place of exchange, is certainly thousands of years old, and by 3000 BC the early city states had large numbers of shops supplying the needs of their inhabitants. Although a major factor in selling was rational gain, how different peoples valued goods was complex and subtle; some articles with little practical use had great social or ceremonial significance in ways that are hard for modern people to grasp. As is the case today, ancient economies were not solely about fulfilling basic needs, but also driven by complex personal desires within the context of the conventions of the time and place – a phenomenon that is of interest to every marketer and salesperson.

MASLOW'S HIERARCHY OF NEEDS

Marketing people were quick to react to the advent of psychology as a subject for serious scientific research in the early twentieth century. The new discipline offered them hope of finding ways to refine and develop their marketing skills. Although many attempts to apply psychology to selling were of questionable effectiveness, in 1943 the psychologist Maslow proposed what was to become a classic theory of motivation, namely his hierarchy of needs (Table 3.1).

Maslow thought that needs form a hierarchy in the sense that people do not try to fulfill higher types of needs before they have satisfied

Table 3.1

Category	Type	
Physical	1. Physiological	Drives for survival, e.g. thirst, hunger
	2. Safety	Health, avoiding physical danger
Social	3. Love and belonging	Being part of a family or a group
	4. Status	Reputation, prestige, fame
Self	5. Self-actualization	Fulfilling one's whole potential

the lower ones. For example, you must satisfy your hunger and make sure you are safe before you start caring about your relationships with others, and so on.

Maslow's idea that the different types of needs have to be satisfied in order has been criticized, but the theory has been useful in understanding how to motivate salespeople. He emphasized that once a need is fulfilled it no longer motivates a person to act, and that people are not all motivated by the same drives at the same time. For the sales manager, identifying what makes individual salespeople "tick" may suggest a customized solution. One salesperson may be performing poorly but have a great need for acceptance by the group – a sales manager may provide the necessary motivation by displaying comparative performance results at team meetings. Another individual may need confidence building, and so on.

THE NINETEENTH CENTURY

The rapid industrialization of leading countries during the nineteenth century ushered in modern marketing and selling methods. Never before had there been such an abundance and variety of goods and services available to so many people. Prior to mass production, the majority of people lived in rural areas and had few opportunities to buy things – itinerant peddlers and regular fairs were the main source of goods, and prices varied considerably from place to place.

In the United States, wholesalers typically collected products from different manufacturers and sold them to jobbers and retailers across their territories. Independent general stores were the main outlet for goods, particularly in rural communities. As prosperity increased, there were many innovations, as follows.

» **1820s**: Retailers in Paris, France, find a way to increase sales to low-income customers by offering goods on installment plans. The item legally belongs to the seller until the last payment is made, but the purchaser can have it for a down payment. The idea travels to the United States, where sewing machines, pianos, and household furnishings are sold on installment plans.

» **1840s**: Branding becomes widely used as a way of distinguishing between competing products, particularly for goods such as wine, where the customer cannot easily test the quality before buying.

» **1841**: The New York retailer A.T. Stewart is thought to have been the first to introduce a one-price system, abolishing the need to bargain and increasing customer goodwill.

» **1843**: P.T. Barnum advertises a free "Grand Buffalo Hunt" in Hoboken, New Jersey, offering people the chance to see the "wild sport of the Western Prairies." The event is a great success, and Barnum makes a fortune from ferry tickets and drink sales. Traveling shows of all kinds serve to alleviate humdrum lives while heavily promoting products such as patent medicines.

» **1859**: The Atlantic and Pacific Tea Company (A&P) standardizes prices and quality for all the merchandise it sells through its own chain of stores. Chain stores find that they can beat the prices of independent retailers by centralized bulk buying, reduced individual service to customers, and efficient management.

» **1870s**: railroad networks create the opportunity for the "traveling salesman" to scour the country for customers. In remoter areas demand is high, and salespeople enjoy far superior market knowledge than their clients.

» **1872**: Montgomery Ward is set up to sell goods to customers living in remote areas through annually produced catalogs. The vast distances in America mean that many people have no access to goods they are eager to buy, and the mail order catalog system is a great success. Sears, Roebuck enters the market in 1886. Copyrighting for catalogs becomes an important skill, and Sears specializes in "product-oriented" copy that assumes the reader has an intimate knowledge of and interest in how things are made. The Sears catalog contains technical drawings of disassembled products and complicated technical descriptions designed for the stingy farmer to read on long winter evenings. By 1907 Sears is distributing 6 million catalogs.

The nineteenth century marks the rise of consumerism and mass marketing techniques, particularly in the United States. The economists of the time argued with little effect that the consumption of "useless luxuries" was wasteful because the money would be better spent investing in useful production that benefitted the whole of society. Governments gradually began to introduce legislation to regulate the quality of goods; in the 1870s, trademark laws were passed in the United States and Britain and some industries, such as champagne makers, began to use the courts to vigorously protect their interests. Installment, or hire purchase, selling was very widespread, but open to abuse due to lack of regulation, as is reflected in the nineteenth-century railroad workers' song "I sold my soul to the company store."

1900–45

In the early part of the twentieth century people's lives were dramatically transformed by innovations such as electric power, the telephone, and the car. Better communications and improvements in mass education led to increasingly effective demands for the democratization of power. One perspective on the two world wars is that they were struggles between competing ideologies that sought to harness the new power of the industrialized worker. Certainly by the end of World War I the old system of government by a small elite was disappearing in the industrialized world.

The new economies were dynamic and unstable, and classical economists failed to show how governments should adapt. The Great Depression of the 1930s was due in large part to competitive devaluations of national currencies around the world and a consequent slump in international trade. Capital "froze" as the wealthy became unwilling to invest in productive industries and millions were out of work.

The Depression was the era of the "hard sell," where salespeople used unscrupulous methods to "slam" their products at customers. The classic negative stereotypes of salespeople and their methods – the "foot in the door," the incomprehensible small print, the fast-talking presentation, inertia selling where unsolicited products are sent out and then billed after a short period – stem from this desperate period.

The British economist J.M. Keynes was the first to challenge the idea that the consumption of luxuries was wasteful. In his book *General Theory of Employment, Interest and Money*, published in 1936, Keynes contended that luxury consumption was highly desirable if it created jobs for the unemployed, pointing out that "the total effect of modern advertising is to shift the preferences of consumers in favor of luxury goods rather than necessities, in favor of consumption rather than saving, and in favor of employment rather than leisure." Keynes practiced what he preached, and was known for gestures such as using all the towels in hotel rooms rather than just one, on the grounds that it created employment for the maids.

1945–70

Keynes' ideas gained acceptance after the war as the allied powers sought to create a world-wide economic system that could cope with the natural instability of industrialization; no one wanted a return to the misery of the 1930s, and it became clear that conspicuous consumption could lead to general prosperity.

Management science, which had been developing steadily since the late nineteenth century, now flourished. Sales and marketing techniques were analyzed, codified, and refined as US business boomed to serve the massive international demand that had been pent up during World War II. With Europe in ruins, US companies had little competition, and salespeople, most of them ex-servicemen, were organized on quasi-military lines. Group training sessions, job security, and strong company loyalty were a feature of a salesman's life in the 1950s.

Ideas that had originally been developed in the nineteenth century by talented businesspeople now became the staple of textbooks and business schools. Every salesperson learned about "prospects," "objections," "needs," "trial closes," and so on. In sales, the emphasis was on persuading the customer to buy during a sales call.

A nineteenth-century innovation in insurance was the insight that it was inefficient to have your top "closers" making repeat calls to collect premiums. The latter task could be performed by less skilled workers. During the 1960s, this idea was extended, especially in business-to-business selling, so that top closers would make the initial sale, and "order takers" would follow up to get repeat business and provide ongoing customer support.

In 1950, Diners Club introduced the first credit card, allowing members to obtain credit at 27 restaurants in New York. The first bank credit card appeared in 1958, but grew slowly, with only 5 million cards in circulation by 1965 – today there are several billion worldwide. Credit cards had a very powerful effect on the US economy, allowing people to purchase much more, and lowering savings rates.

As Europe and Japan recovered from the war, their economies and consumption patterns began to "Americanize." Marketing methods developed in the United States gained increasing acceptance elsewhere.

1970–THE PRESENT

The oil shocks of the 1970s were a wake-up call to the West to change some of its wasteful ways, and became a catalyst for many social changes. People began to care more about their health, their lifestyle, and so on, while young people with money to spend became a hugely important new market.

Increasing labor costs and overheads began to drive developed world manufacturers overseas, a process that continues to this day in the face of strongly resistant special interest groups. Sophisticated multinationals have developed with enormous international buying power, and many suppliers have specialized in "key account management," selling to a few large customers' special needs. It can be a risky business, but for the salesperson the focus is on teamwork and quality issues, rather than the traditional emphasis on closing a sale with every call.

Marketing has become more sophisticated, and so have consumers, who are better informed than ever before. Outside retail stores, personal selling to consumers is now concentrated in a handful of high-priced items that justify the expense of personal attention.

The IT revolution has thrown many supply chains into disarray, but many of the fears that the Internet would put "bricks and mortar" companies out of business have proved unfounded. A business is more than its channels, it seems – expert knowledge of its customers, its products, and the ability to provide services have stood up to the challenge of the initial dotcom wave very well, and it is now learning from its new rival's mistakes.

While the essential art of selling remains perennially the same, tactics and methods continue to alter according to circumstances. Survival in sales has always meant having the willingness to change, and will continue to do so in the future.

TIMELINE

» **1820s**: Parisian retailers introduce the installment plan.
» **1840s**: Branding becomes widely used.
» **1841**: New York retailer A.T. Stewart starts a one-price system. No more haggling!
» **1859**: The Atlantic and Pacific Tea Company (A&P) uses efficient management and centralized buying to create the first modern chain store where all goods are standardized.
» **1870s**: Traveling salesmen exploit railroad travel to reach remote customers.
» **1870s**: Trademark legislation introduced, long after trademarks have become standard commercial practice.
» **1872**: Montgomery Ward, the first mail order catalog company, is founded.
» **1886**: Sears, Roebuck founded, introducing the highly readable, product-oriented mail order catalog.
» **1916**: Henry Ford offers cars on hire purchase plans.
» **1930s**: The Great Depression. Millions are out of work world-wide and investors turn away from industry. Salespeople use hard-sell tactics and unethical methods to combat falling turnover.
» **1936**: Publication of *General Theory of Employment, Interest and Money*, by J.M. Keynes, which proposes that the consumption of luxuries can create employment.
» **1950s/60s**: The US-dominated postwar boom supplies a huge world-wide demand, pent up by the deprivations of World War II. Sales theory and training become institutionalized.
» **1970s**: The energy crisis has wide ramifications across many industries as people seek to reduce their energy costs.
» **1980s**: Financial deregulation and the lowering of trade barriers boost development overseas, particularly in Asia. Manufacturers begin to move their factories to lower-cost countries.
» **1990s – the present**: Due to the high cost of selling, most sales-people work in business-to-business selling, where supply has become increasingly sophisticated and efficient. The collapse of the

USSR and the end of the Cold War open vast new markets, and most companies realize that the main opportunities for growth lie in the developing world.

KEY LEARNING POINTS

» The ability to sell is very ancient, but the skills and approaches that are effective vary greatly according to culture, circumstances, and value systems. There is no single "right" way to sell something, only ways that are appropriate at the time.

» Psychologists such as Maslow have sought to understand elusive human qualities such as motivation. Sensitive marketers and salespeople have found various ways to apply these insights.

» Most of the modern ways of doing business have their origins in the nineteenth century, when rapid industrialization created massive new markets for goods of all kinds. Branding, advertising, public relations, sales training, product standardization, copywriting, hire purchase, and personal selling in the field are all approaches that were used successfully in the nineteenth century.

» The nineteenth century saw the birth of mass consumerism, which was generally disapproved of by the ruling classes. People worried that consumerism led to waste.

» Two world wars and the Great Depression completely changed the way people live. By the end of World War II, it was understood that consumerism was a route to productivity and high employment.

» Easier credit in the United States provides an enormous boost to business. Savings rates drop as people begin to buy with credit cards.

» In the 1950s and 1960s, business becomes a science, and selling techniques that were first tried in the nineteenth century are taught in thousands of business courses around the world.

» By the 1980s, governments perceive the need to loosen the reins on business to stay competitive. Privatization and deregulation are the order of the day, leading to new sales opportunities.

- The end of the Cold War opens up the Soviet bloc to Western-style capitalism. Globalization becomes a buzzword as firms rush to establish themselves internationally. Growth in the developed world seems restricted to new technologies, but they prove to be highly volatile.

The E-Dimension

» IT in sales
» The promise of CRM
» The reality
» Best practice: Barclays.

Despite the widespread failure of direct selling via the Web during the Internet boom of the late 1990s, the Internet has subsequently become an integral part of sales for many companies. It is best understood in the context of the rapid adoption of IT in all aspects of business: e-commerce can no longer be seen narrowly as a stand-alone sales channel. Web presence, e-mail, mobile telephony, telemarketing, EPOS (electronic point of sale), DDE (direct data entry), and new generations of computer software for planning and analysis are being used in concert to open up opportunities for productivity gains in sales.

The chief benefits of the Internet to consumers are:

» Comparison shopping – customers can rapidly obtain and compare specifications and prices for competing products from their own homes.
» Better use of time – many consumers resent time spent dealing with poorly trained sales staff and use the Internet to minimize this.
» Convenience – the Internet is open 24 hours a day for both information and, to a lesser degree, purchasing.
» Multimedia presentation – well-designed multimedia pages combining video, sound, and photographs can be more effective as a buying aid than a brochure.

The chief benefits to firms are:

» Quick updating of brochures as Internet Web pages.
» 24-hour display of goods and services.
» Lower costs in distribution, printing, and order processing.
» Direct contact with the consumer for manufacturers.
» More potential for bespoke products (Dell Computers, for example, offers customers the facility to "design" their own system online).
» Better relationships with customers.
» Potentially a global reach.
» Better market research.

IT IN SALES

IT applications, including the Internet, have transformed internal company processes:

» Salespeople can access company computers remotely while they are in the field.
» E-mail dramatically speeds up communications.
» Time management software.
» Database files.
» Desktop publishing.
» Account management and sales management software.
» Importance of intelligent use.

ACCIDENTAL INDUSTRIAL ESPIONAGE

In 1995 I was in Hong Kong for a week negotiating a major contract with a customer. It was clear that he was hedging his bets, and I suspected that this was because he had other suppliers who were in competition with our company, which is small, employing only 20 people. I'm not particularly computer literate, and I'd had problems in the past using my laptop in foreign hotel rooms to access e-mails – sometimes the charges are very high. So on the first evening, I used the hotel's computer to send some personal e-mails, and had to save some files temporarily on the hard drive.

When I came to delete them, I noticed that there were some other files left in the "My Briefcase" folder by other guests. One of them bore the name of my Hong Kong customer. I couldn't resist the temptation to open it. It was amazing – it was a draft contract between my customer and a foreign firm with which we had distribution arrangements, laying out a detailed plan for entering our own market. There was also correspondence between the firm's negotiator – who was evidently still in town – and his head office that referred to its concerns that we might get wind of the deal, which, as they were clearly aware, was in flagrant breach of our distribution agreement.

I e-mailed the material to my managing director and called that night to discuss matters. The next day, she had our lawyer fax a threatening letter to our distributor, suggesting that we would sue them if they were to breach our agreements. Meanwhile, the local customer was all smiles, and the following afternoon and evening were spent in lavish entertainment, but no discussion of business. When I arrived at his office on the day after, however, he was ready to sign the deal; there was no mention of my competitor, but it was obvious that the lawyer's letter had worked and the competitor had pulled out.

In the late 1990s the development of the World Wide Web engendered great optimism that the connectivity it offered, combined with new software, would transform the selling function beyond recognition.

THE PROMISE OF CRM

Pundits confidently predicted that soon all major businesses would be using integrated software packages that would automate the "front office" so that enquiries, orders, and meetings with customers could be largely conducted over the Internet. "Enterprise software," "customer relationship management" (CRM) tools, and "sales force automation" (SFA) would reduce the number of staff a company needed while massively increasing productivity. E-mail and offshore call centres would replace traditional customer interfaces and suppliers and customers would use the same software to transmit information instantaneously along the supply chain.

CRM allows the salesperson on the road to use a laptop or palmtop to:

» View and update critical customer data.
» Add new contacts and opportunities.
» Take notes.
» Assign tasks.
» Check and update the calendar.
» Forecast revenues accurately.
» Track leads.
» Follow deals through the pipeline.
» Calculate performance metrics for individuals and teams.
» Collaborate more easily with other sales team members.
» Have real-time, company-wide access to detailed account data.
» Analyse market trends at will.

In addition, sales managers can:

» Maintain more accurate forecasts and view them from various perspectives.
» View active, but locked forecasts.
» Lock forecasts.
» View the same forecasts as sales staff.
» View projected revenue and shadow forecasts that will be credited to a sales rep.
» Simplify the quote and order processes.
» Plan and manage territories proactively.

By giving intermediaries and retailers access to product data online using passwords, CRM can make it easier and quicker for them to get the information they need, since the database can be viewed 24 hours a day and, in theory, is always up to date. Information about channel partners' activities and product interests can be fed back to the sales force to help them make more accurate forecasts and to plan their presentations (if you know that the staff of Customer X have been investigating new Product A on the database, you can emphasize Product A's benefits on your next call).

The scope for improving sales support activities is substantial. Without CRM, customers often find themselves having to explain their situation every time they call, and often cannot get up-to-date answers about matters that are currently being processed, such as returns, repairs, replacements, and order despatch. If the salesperson calls without being informed of these events, the customer starts complaining about the unresolved issue and the selling opportunity evaporates. CRM enables teleworkers at call centres to have access to the instantly updated customer data, allowing them to answer queries in a more personalized way – no more "I'm sorry, I'll have to check with despatch and call you back." At the same time, salespeople can discover exactly what has been going on between customers and support staff, and can plan their call accordingly. Customers love to deal with reps who are completely up to date with sales support issues.

In 1995 and 1996, software companies were falling over each other to get a piece of this enormous new market – there was a torrent of IPOs (Initial Public Offerings) on the stock market and acquisitions as pundits confidently predicted industry sales of over $30 billion by 2002. Every firm would need some form of Web-enabled software, and there were hundreds of competing products. The name of the game was to offer total integration of business processes, customized to the individual firm's needs. Systems in the accounts department, warehouse, and marketing groups would all be linked, providing a seamless flow of information that would allow firms, for the first time, to communicate consistent messages to customers and suppliers; whatever was known by one part of the firm would be known by all the others.

THE REALITY

It all sounded so good, but as with so many innovations in IT, the vision was far ahead of the actual capabilities of the software and programmers' understanding of what firms really need. As Erin Kinikin, a vice-president at the Giga Information Group, remarked in an article entitled "Eight Myths of CRM": "Setting complete integration as the first priority for CRM is akin to proposing 'world peace' as the first step to help the poor."

CRM software is supposed to help salespeople plan, schedule, and control sales activities, thus increasing revenue while reducing costs. All of the major enterprise software vendors, such as Oracle, SAP, PeopleSoft, and Microsoft offer CRM packages, but, at the time of writing, customers are becoming increasingly vocal in expressing their dissatisfaction. Most CRM money is spent on the technology, yet using it effectively requires massive organizational change that may be undesirable. Salespeople have shown marked resistance to requirements to input all their information about leads into the system – in part, perhaps, for competitive reasons, but also because the constant juggling of hardware, the need to learn how to operate the programs, and the irritation of yet more form filling just seem like a waste of time. While sales support can be automated successfully, it now seems that front line reps are better left to do what they are good at – selling.

Confidence in the whole idea of knowledge management, the process of getting the "wetware" in people's minds recorded so that others can use it, has diminished. The overconfident abstractions of software developers – the "world peace" syndrome – have encountered natural limits. Records are no substitute for training, experience, and expertise, and nobody wants to spend large amounts of time inputting their personal knowledge into a company-wide database; furthermore, the time it takes to implement a new system – measured in years rather than months – increases the difficulties as the business environment changes. Speed is at a premium during a boom when everybody is racing to grab as much of the sales pie as they can, but during a downturn firms have to work smarter, not faster.

Embarrassingly, there is increasing evidence that many companies that have implemented the new systems are finding that many of their staff are not using them. Some researchers suggest that 25% of CRM systems have already been abandoned by firms, at a huge cost. According to Robert Desisto, a vice-president at research firm Gartner, "Applying technology to the salesperson, quite frankly, has been a big disappointment." According to Desisto, as much as 50% of all future CRM implementations will be viewed as failures. Salespeople have been particularly resistant to the requirement that they input large amounts of information, often on the grounds that there was no benefit to themselves as individuals, and sanctions, such as withholding commissions until all the information is supplied, are not working, especially when the salespeople are high achievers – the company needs them more than they need the company, and they know it. Often CRM is the pet project of one or two executives and if they leave, people start to ignore the system.

BEST PRACTICE: BARCLAYS

The unusual complexity of financial products offers considerable potential for efficiency gains by applying CRM – selling large loans, such as house mortgages, can be as difficult as selling insurance, since applications are often refused by the credit department. In Britain deregulation of financial services has increased the competition among lenders, and any bureaucratic delays encourage borrowers to switch to another lender who offers smoother processing.

At Barclays Bank, mortgage sales teams were eager to have the capacity to make a firm offer of a loan early in the selling process on the grounds that this would increase closing rates. Like the other major British banks, Barclays owns a very rich database of customer information, but sales staff did not have easy or quick access to it. In the field, sellers did not always have a terminal to hand, so a more ubiquitous solution was needed.

In 2000 Barclays set up a trial where 25 sales staff could telephone a "credit data warehouse" by mobile phone or from a land line 24 hours a day. The warehouse holds pre-approved mortgage credit limits for some 3.5 million individuals. The seller speaks a PIN number and staff number for security, the sort code of the sales outlet, and the client's customer number. A computerized voice then informs the seller of the customer's credit limit, based on information that is updated monthly.

The trial proved a success, cutting sales presentation times by up to 30 minutes and generating an extra £1 million in sales in two months. The system was then extended to 4000 salespeople around the country, increasing the conversion rates by 5% and increasing sales by £70 million in the first six months of the roll-out. Furthermore, the cost of the system was recouped during the same period.

A cautious and well-focused approach to the application – and no attempt at total integration of business processes – yielded a very satisfactory result for everyone concerned. The sales force got what they wanted – the ability to make a firm offer immediately – while customers obtained quick service in a process which can often be nerve-wrackingly slow and uncertain.

Source: "Giving Voice to Customer-Centricity Reaps Big ROI for Barclays", www.sas.com

KEY LEARNING POINTS

» CRM and other Web-enabled software designed to automate sales and marketing processes were oversold during the 1990s. Vendors with the "world peace" syndrome promised total integration of a company's systems and even envisioned industry-wide systems along whole supply chains. Within a few years, many companies began to abandon the systems because they were proving unworkable.

» For sales support processes, however, CRM and its relatives are proving effective. Call centres manned by staff with all the customer's information at their fingertips are providing more efficient and timely service, while salespeople can check on support issues quickly and easily.

» For salespeople, being able to access brochures, product information, prices and delivery time, and customer account information at any time is clearly beneficial. Customized solutions to industry-specific problems, such as those of Barclays loan sellers, need to able to offer instant loan approval, and are also likely to be welcomed by sales teams. Rigid all-embracing systems requiring sales people to enter enormous amounts of information, on the other hand, are likely to be resisted vigorously.

The Global Dimension

- » Indirect selling overseas
- » Licensing
- » Export houses
- » Agents
- » Distributors
- » Direct selling
- » Pricing
- » Culture
- » Best practice: Dyson.

The enormous opportunities and challenges of selling world-wide are discussed in detail in the ExpressExec title *Global Sales*. In this chapter we will examine the basic issues facing exporters.

There are two main opportunities for companies to sell overseas: the unavailability of a product in an overseas market and differentiation in products and services.

» Product unavailability: Most commodities are only found in some parts of the world; Britain, for instance, must import items such as coffee, bananas, and rubber from tropical regions because they cannot be produced at home. Similarly, high-tech products that rely on a sophisticated infrastructure cannot be produced in many countries, so they must be imported from elsewhere. Patent protection may also have the same effect – cutting-edge pharmaceutical products are principally generated in the United States and parts of Europe, but world-wide patent protection is often obtained. Short of flouting international trade agreements (an issue in the pharmaceutical world), other countries are forced to purchase such drugs from the foreign patent holders.

» Differentiation: Many industries, such as fast food and car manufacturing, have an array of brand-name products that customers regard as different from one another, on the grounds of quality, price, service, or more intangible reasons. Most countries that are major car manufacturers, for example, nevertheless import foreign-made vehicles.

Within these broad categories, there are a host of more specific reasons for firms to sell abroad, such as:

» A fast-growing foreign market.
» Losing market share at home.
» Products that may be reaching the end of their life-span at home may be in demand in less developed countries.
» To hedge against a possible domestic economic downturn.
» Possessing specialized expertise that does not exist in a foreign market.
» To gain economies of scale at home and abroad by expanding total production
» To "dump" surplus stock or to use excess production capacity.

In general, entering a foreign market entails higher expenses and greater risks. A firm must decide whether to sell directly (often the highest risk and greatest profit potential) or indirectly through intermediaries. Most firms begin by using indirect methods.

INDIRECT SELLING OVERSEAS

Overseas agents and distributors are thought to handle more than 50% of the world's overseas trade. Along with licensing and export houses, these intermediaries are often the most cost-effective method of selling abroad. There is no universal solution – a company generally must tailor-make its arrangements to suit its needs in each market that it enters. Many countries have a strong demand for products and services but have high import barriers or political instability that make it impossible or too risky to sell direct – Thailand's customs offices, for example, are notoriously difficult toward newcomers.

LICENSING

Firms may choose to license the right to manufacture a product where:

» the cost of transporting the finished goods from the home country is too high (e.g. low-value, heavy items);
» the pace of change to the product is very fast (e.g. personal computers);
» the country has a track record of seizing foreign-owned assets;
» there is a danger that the country may forbid repatriating profits; or
» the firm lacks the capital to set up a factory overseas.

As with all intermediaries, picking the right licensee is essential. The primary risk of licensing is that royalties may not be paid. One strategy to protect against this is to insist on supplying key components that can be withheld if debts are not paid.

Licensing involves granting a foreign company the patent or trademark rights to sell or make its products in the territory. It is attractive to small and medium-sized companies because it does not require much investment, but it is certainly the least profitable way to access a foreign market.

EXPORT HOUSES

Export houses are generally based in the home country and handle all or part of the overseas selling for firms who are selling to a given market on a small scale. Typically they offer a range of services, including:

» selecting agents and distributors;
» providing market information;
» dealing with export documentation;
» supervising sales activities of agents and distributors; and
» handling export finance and credit.

Companies may choose to use an export house where:

» they lack marketing know-how;
» the export house has specialized capabilities in a particular country or industry; and
» the cost of entering the market is prohibitive.

Using an export house adds an extra layer to the chain of intermediaries, with the obvious disadvantage that the producing firm has little contact with its foreign market and may not be able to monitor market developments adequately.

AGENTS

Agents are commonly independent operators, getting orders for the exporter in return for commission.

There is a common conflict of interest between agents and exporters that needs to be handled with foresight: agents know that as they generate more business for the exporter, the incentive for the exporter to bypass them and enter the market directly increases. Agents may attempt to protect themselves by gathering agencies for a large number of competing exporters, or by failing to exploit the market as thoroughly as possible. Many exporters seek to defuse this problem by either agreeing on a gradual run-down of the agency agreement as sales increase, or by guaranteeing a long-term arrangement for a fixed period. A good agent may be in a position to assist in the eventual establishment of a subsidiary in the country, so many firms take the view that it is good business to deal with agents fairly.

DISTRIBUTORS

Unlike agents, distributors purchase from the exporter for resale in their territory. This usually involves a higher volume of business, with potential cost savings on bulk transportation. They are legally responsible for the trade in their markets and provide their own financing.

From the exporters' perspective, a common problem with distributors is that they control the selling price in their market. If price is a critical factor, exporters should only deal with distributors who will agree on a fixed margin and retail price, but this has to be monitored closely.

Unlike agents, distributors actually purchase the goods, but it is important not to treat them as just another customer. Developing a close relationship, and providing as much technical and marketing support as possible, is the key to success. Information flow should be in both directions, with the distributor feeding back market information as much as possible.

DIRECT SELLING

Opening a subsidiary or selling direct gives an exporter far greater control over its foreign market at the price of increased costs and higher risk.

In the case of subsidiaries, sometimes set up as joint ventures between two or more exporters, the exporter must decide whether to make the subsidiary simply a marketing organization or whether establishing a local factory is justified. Much depends on the political climate, labor laws, tax regime, and so on. With bulky or heavy products, freight costs can be reduced by starting a local assembly plant; providing local employment generally creates goodwill and helps to deepen ties to the market.

The following factors are important in deciding whether or not to take the manufacturing route.

» Can the foreign market be adequately served from the home production facility?
» Will the foreign government allow the firm to repatriate profits? Is it liable to change its mind in the future? Even in the current era of free global capital flows, there are still many cases of expropriation,

for example Zimbabwe's recent seizure of farms owned by people of European extraction.

» Are grants available? Will a local plant circumvent high import tariffs or non-tariff barriers such as costly safety and packaging regulations for imports?

Joint ventures

Joint ventures involve collaboration with one or more foreign firms. This approach is increasing in popularity, partly due to reduced economic and political risks. The great advantage is a "ready-made" partner's distribution system, and the fact that this may be the only way to gain access to foreign markets. The danger is that the partners may not cooperate effectively, leading to a costly process of disentanglement.

Direct selling

Sending home-country salespeople overseas to close orders is attractive because it cuts out intermediaries and requires no capital investment. This approach can work when:

» There is a high-value product that is tailor-made for the individual customer, such as a machine.
» The product is technically complex, requiring training and after-sales support that only the manufacturer can provide.
» The buyer requires a continuous supply, and only needs occasional visits from salespeople to negotiate prices and discuss problems.
» The buyer is in a neighboring country that is easy to serve from home.

Sales people should have a good knowledge of the buyer's country and market, and should preferably speak the buyer's local language. Normally it takes a long time to nurture the relationship and build up trust. Many firms invite buyers to visit their offices at home and provide incentives in the form of expense-paid business meetings and conferences in attractive locations. In some developing countries, these perks can be extensive and central to achieving a sale – in China, for example, it is common for buyers and officials to ask overseas firms for financial help in family matters, such as sending their children to study overseas. While such payments could constitute bribery, the reality is that in some countries there is simply no other way to do business, and anti-bribery legislation in the West tends to recognize this fact of life (see the title *Global Sales*, Chapter 6, "Corruption").

PRICING

Freight

Selling overseas usually entails higher freight costs and special packaging. Exporters often accept a low profit margin in order to keep their overseas prices competitive despite the increased costs.

Tariffs and other barriers

One of the few issues that almost all economists agree on is that tariffs restrict trade and ultimately damage the importing country's economy. According to the theory of free trade, it is not necessary for countries to negotiate tariff reductions with other nations; simply abolish your own tariffs unilaterally, say economists, and your country's prosperity will increase as international business floods in. Consumers benefit directly because they ultimately bear the cost of all import duties.

Despite the convincing arguments for free trade, politicians have great difficulty in implementing such a regime, even if they pay lip service to doing so. Powerful lobbies at home are eager to protect their own interests, while employees of inefficient local firms and industries are often violently resistant to the changes that free markets bring. The United States, for instance, is often seen as the champion of free trade, yet it protects domestic industries such as sugar and textiles, keeping prices artificially high, for no sound economic reason. In developing countries, tariffs are often portrayed as a way of preventing predatory foreigners from exploiting local people, but such arguments are generally spurious.

Non-tariff barriers come in many forms and often appear superficially to be there for good reasons, such as safety. In many cases, they are really there to slow down or prevent foreign imports.

Exporters have to accept these uncomfortable realities and recognize that trade barriers are unlikely ever to disappear entirely. Since there is a hidden agenda to most barriers, it is vital to have extensive local knowledge and be in close touch with any potential changes. Often, having a local partner is the only way to ensure that products actually manage to make it through the system and into the country. Salespeople who are unaware of these problems often become frustrated at their firm's reluctance to enter what appears to be a lucrative foreign market – your boss may know something about the situation that you don't! In Thailand, for example, established importers have been known to bribe customs officials to prevent competitors' products from entering the country. In circumstances like this, a new entrant needs to prepare the ground very carefully before making any firm commitments.

Transfer pricing

Since duties and taxes vary greatly around the world, international firms have the opportunity to concentrate processes in low-cost countries to maximize profits. For example, a firm may choose to import components from one country into another to minimize import duties and assemble the final product locally, or transfer products across borders at very high prices to minimize corporation tax in the end country. The scope for manipulating these internal "transfer prices" is very great, and customs and tax authorities actively try to prevent abuses. In a truly globalized free trade environment, of course, transfer pricing would be unnecessary.

CULTURE

Inexperienced sellers often assume that a foreign market is very similar to their own. This is almost never the case, with cultural factors affecting almost every aspect of business, from what "Yes" means (it can vary in meaning from a simple affirmative to "maybe," "I'll ask my boss," or even "I don't want to embarrass either of us by saying no"), how products are perceived, and different perceptions of what constitutes an "Act of God" in insurance claims, to how one should behave at meetings. Although almost everyone in international business across the world recognizes the problem of cultural differences and does their best to overcome them, the influence can subtly disrupt even the friendliest transactions. Much useful academic research has been done in this area in recent years, and the ExpressExec title *Global Sales* explores the issues in detail.

BEST PRACTICE: DYSON

Manufacturing in high-wage countries such as those in Western Europe is becoming increasingly difficult to sustain. In Britain, for example, manufacturing shed 150,000 jobs in 2000 as its output shrank by 5.4% and its share of national economic activity fell below 20%. The country now adds value in its service industries, such as banking, restaurants, and call centres, which added almost 230,000 jobs in the same year. To economists, the transition is a necessary part of global industrial development, and the country as a whole does not lose out by entering new businesses. Manufacturing workers, however, are often reluctant to retrain and seek new careers in expanding sectors of the economy while their former employers relocate their plants in Asia, which supplies cheap labor for foreign factories and also encourages outsourcing contracts awarded by multinationals to local firms.

In 1978 British designer and inventor James Dyson conceived of a new type of vacuum cleaner that used centrifugal force to separate dirt from air rather than using bags and filters. After developing thousands of prototypes with his own money, Dyson approached the major firms in the industry, such as Electrolux, Philips, and Black & Decker, but was unable to make a deal.

According to his lawyer, trying to interest the industry in what Dyson claims to be a superior machine was "like extracting teeth." Dyson borrowed £600,000 to manufacture and market his patented "Dual Cyclone" cleaner and scoured Europe for potential licensees without success.

The big breakthrough came in 1991 when Dyson won the 1991 International Design Fair Prize in Japan and launched the product under license. It rapidly became a status symbol there, selling for $2000 per unit. Other coups followed, such as when fashion designer Sir Paul Smith introduced it in his upmarket British clothes shop. Using the Japanese license royalties, Dyson began to make a new model in Britain, opening a plant in Wiltshire in 1993.

By the following year, his top-selling model was the biggest selling vacuum cleaner in Britain. As local and international sales mushroomed, Dyson encountered a brutal response from some of his larger competitors, including patent infringement (winning a legal battle against Hoover in 2002) and constant claims that his machine was not better at suction.

Dyson currently has more than 40% of the British market, is the best-selling vacuum cleaner in Australia and New Zealand, and is preparing to enter the United States for the first time.

Britain's strong currency and unwillingness to join the euro caused problems, however, and in 2002 James Dyson told the BBC that "the pound is overvalued by 30%. When we export we are 30% more expensive." Beating forthcoming EU legislation intended to prevent firms from relocating overseas, Dyson announced his intention to move part of his production facility to Malaysia and axe 800 jobs at the Wiltshire factory. He intends to keep his production of innovative washing machines and the Research and Development Unit in Britain because of the danger of industrial espionage, but sees reducing costs as essential if he is to penetrate the cut-throat US market in the future. Malaysian factory workers earn about £3 an hour, compared with British workers' £9, while Malaysian office rents are about a third of those in Britain.

In Britain, debate over the move (Dyson is one of the largest firms owned by a single individual) divided along predictable lines: to small businesspeople, James Dyson is a hero who has beaten Britain's "anti-entrepreneurial" system, while to unions and local lobbyists, relocation is a selfish act that destroys workers' lives in the pursuit of profit.

KEY LEARNING POINTS

» With the industrializing countries representing the largest opportunities for growth, selling overseas is becoming a necessity for many firms, particularly in manufacturing, but exporting is both riskier and more expensive than expanding at home.

» Most companies try to reduce risk when first entering a foreign market at the cost of reduced profits; licensing is often the easiest way to begin, followed by agency agreements, distribution deals where the distributor purchases the product, and finally by setting up overseas subsidiaries to market and/or manufacture goods locally.

» A major problem for exporters is local trade barriers, and careful research is needed to ensure that an apparently promising market is actually accessible – the high cost of barriers, such as tariffs, may make entry uneconomic.

The State of the Art

- » Key account management (KAM)
- » How KAM develops
- » Global account management (GAM) in the PC industry
- » The Huthwaite approach to KAM selling
- » Relationship selling and the "Quality" movement
- » Sales recruitment
- » Researching your potential employers.

KEY ACCOUNT MANAGEMENT (KAM)

While the trend in business buying is toward centralization, the cost of maintaining a sales force in the field is increasing in real terms. One response to this situation is to focus on a small number of large customers – across many industries, firms are finding that as much as 70% of their business sales come from a handful of clients. This has made key account management (KAM), the special treatment of important business customers, increase in importance.

Key accounts – sometimes referred to as "national accounts" or "global accounts" – tend to have complex needs because they are large organizations with many operating units and decision makers spread across different locations. The strategy is to develop long-term partnerships where the customer overtly designates the seller as a "preferred supplier" and where the staff of the two firms interact constantly. Usually many salespeople are involved in managing a key account, requiring efficient lines of communication and coordination.

For the supplier, a successful relationship with a key account offers:

» The chance to share research and development costs with the buyer.
» Reduced costs because of close cooperation in planning production and delivery cycles.
» Higher, and firmer, sales.
» A more secure career path for the salesforce.
» An easier selling process because of less resistance to sales calls.
» The chance to provide better sales support and after-sales service.

On the other hand, KAM carries some risk.

» The supplier is dependent on a small number of major customers. If one or two stop buying, turnover and profit are dramatically cut.
» Major customers may attempt to squeeze the supplier's profit margins or demand ever more costly services.
» The supplier may not pay enough attention to smaller accounts that have better growth potential in the long term.
» High-performing salespeople may find the cooperative approach to selling too restricting and leave to pursue more challenging opportunities elsewhere.

HOW KAM DEVELOPS

KAM does not happen overnight; usually the supplier has had a business relationship with the customer for many years and has an intimate knowledge of the company. As KAM is essentially a selling strategy, the question of whether a particular customer should be groomed for key account status has to be thought through carefully and non-starters should be ruled out early. Where the firm identifies a customer with KAM potential, it often invests in improving services and product availability before making the initial approach and makes a special effort to understand the nature of its relationship with competing suppliers. Often, the opportunity to establish KAM arises when a competing supplier lets the customer down in some way.

Convincing the customer of the advantages of KAM is not usually easy, and the supplier needs to have an intimate understanding of how decisions are made in the target company, as well as problems that it has that the supplier could help to alleviate. Consistent performance and the development of trust are essential.

If the customer is willing to try a weak form of KAM, such as agreeing to regard the supplier as a preferred source, relationships between staff in the two companies can be deepened by more joint meetings and even social events. The supplier seeks to involve senior managers in the target company as much as possible.

If the relationship is successful, the firms may sign a formal contract committing them to a partnership lasting several years. This implies a high level of trust, since they will share commercially sensitive information. Performance targets are agreed and monitored jointly, and the focus is on collaborative problem solving and product development and mutual staff training. The customer buys all or most of the relevant products from the supplier in return for guaranteed continuity of supply and high quality standards.

The final stage of KAM is where the two firms behave almost as if they are part of a single entity. Senior executives hold joint meetings to plan strategies and costs are transparent – the two companies keep no secrets from one another. The relationship may ultimately result in a merger.

GLOBAL ACCOUNT MANAGEMENT (GAM) IN THE PC INDUSTRY

Selling to the semiconductor industry is extremely complex, with long sales cycles, huge numbers of staff located world-wide, and opaque decision-making processes that few outsiders can fathom.

Many of the major international manufacturers of semiconductors and integrated circuits ask their suppliers to set up "global account management teams" to service their highly specialized needs across the world. Firms such as Intel, IBM, Motorola, and NEC have so much buying power that they can insist upon the arrangement, which some suppliers try to resist. In this rapidly changing industry, manufacturers need to optimize their capacity to transfer the production process to any of their plants across the world as fast as possible and at low cost. Furthermore, they are seeking to establish consistent prices globally for their supplies.

Although having such a close relationship with a major manufacturer should lead to large and predictable sales, smaller suppliers are at a disadvantage. Not only may a very large customer squeeze profit margins and require ever more complex services, but arrogant individuals may make arbitrary demands that can be extremely costly for the supplier. Setting up a global account management (GAM) team requires considerable investment, and suppliers need to protect themselves carefully. When GAM works, however, it allows suppliers to sell effectively to all of the customer's factories world-wide; an intimate technical knowledge of the customer's present and future needs is critical in the industry, and the close ties of GAM give the supplier a huge selling advantage over its competitors. Suppliers come to know the customer's corporate culture, its business strategies, and the character of key individuals within the firm at a level of detail that would be impossible for an outsider. Being a preferred supplier to a multinational is also great advertising: other potential customers are likely to be impressed.

KAM can break down at any point in the process. Often breakdowns occur because of personal conflicts between individuals, especially in the early stages. Another common cause of breakdown is that the supplier has failed to build a high enough barrier to entry; changes in the industry may allow competitors to offer superior products. This is one reason why joint research and development can be important – the supplier should seek to tailor its products as perfectly as possible to the customer's needs. It is not always the buyer that breaks the relationship, however. Sometimes changes in the market or poor performance by the buyer will convince the seller that KAM is no longer appropriate.

THE HUTHWAITE APPROACH TO KAM SELLING

So how does selling to a key account differ from normal "transactional" selling?

The British firm Huthwaite Research Group, inventors of the SPIN strategy (see below), suggest a four-stage model for the KAM sales call, as follows.

Preliminary

Establish who the seller is, why it is there, and obtain "permission" to ask the buyer questions. Huthwaite finds that while no specific opening approach is significantly superior, successful salespeople tend to use a wider variety of approaches.

Investigation

Huthwaite sees this stage as the key to success in selling to key accounts. The seller asks the buyer questions, both to find out its needs and to discover information about the company. Huthwaite's founder Neil Rackham distinguishes between explicit needs, such as when the customer says "I need a new photocopier," and implied needs, where the customer complains about a problem "Our photocopiers are no good." The salesperson's challenge is to lead the customer from the implied need to an explicit recognition of that need.

SPIN selling

SPIN, a registered trademark of the Huthwaite Research Group, is an acronym standing for Situation, Problem, Implication, and Need–pay-off, used to describe the stages of questioning used to lead customers to the point where they are willing to discuss seller's solutions and benefits. Having obtained permission to ask the customer questions, the salesperson begins by probing the current situation and then asks questions designed to elicit statements of dissatisfaction, such as "Is the machine reliable?" With larger sales, Rackham points out that the purchaser is taking a personal risk – if the company is not satisfied, the purchaser will be blamed. For this reason SPIN's "Implication" stage is designed to build up a feeling that the problem is serious – so serious that it is worth taking the risk of purchasing a new solution. Implication questions are intended to persuade the customer to contemplate how, say, the faulty photocopier leads to many unsatisfactory consequences (poorly copied reports for board meetings etc.). The presentation concludes with "Need-payoff" questions that focus on the solution to the problems that the customer agrees exist, for example "How would a faster color photocopier benefit you?" These questions also help to "rehearse" customers for internal meetings where they must promote or defend the purchase. "Need-payoff" questions focus only on solutions that the salesperson can actually offer.

Perhaps the most important insight of the SPIN system is the need to rehearse and stage-manage customers' internal meetings where the salesperson cannot be present. With key accounts, the level of trust allows a closer interaction with customer staff, allowing the seller greater opportunity to ensure that the customer can successfully "sell" the proposed purchase to colleagues.

Demonstration

Once the customer states an explicit need, the salesperson can show how the product provides the solution. If the need is only implied, the buyer can object to the solution on the grounds of cost – "I don't want to pay thousands of dollars just to solve that" – so Huthwaite encourages sellers to build up the problem in the customers' minds to the point where they clearly state the need, for example "I want a photocopier that we can run 6 hours a day without problems and an inexpensive service contract with a same-day repair guarantee; that's worth paying \$X for."

Commitment

Instead of trying to close a sale to a key account, Rackham argues that it is better to aim at establishing a commitment on some action point that moves the process along, such as persuading the customer to attend a demonstration or to allow access to a higher level decision maker.

RELATIONSHIP SELLING AND THE "QUALITY" MOVEMENT

The remarkable success of Japanese manufacturing during the postwar period made Western companies, particularly in the United States, pay close attention to their production methods. W. Edwards Deming of the Ford Motor Company used his studies of Japanese companies to develop an influential theory of quality management during the 1970s that led to the introduction of company "quality circles," committees that met to explore ways of improving quality standards.

Originally a philosophy of manufacturing, the "Quality" movement is now an important part of selling. Globalization is forcing marketing departments to take a longer term view of their operations, and to focus on developing enduring relationships with their major customers rather than simply viewing sales as a series of one-off transactions. In the auto industry, for example, manufacturers have very close relationships with their dealers, often supplying training, showroom floor plans, merchandising support, and a host of other services to build and maintain their brands. "Just-in-time" (JIT) management, introduced by Toyota, focuses on customer needs and aims to meet those needs as quickly as possible while minimizing inventory levels along the whole supply chain. In JIT firms, and also among retailers, buyers often take the initiative in seeking sellers (so-called "reverse marketing"), the focus being on quality and consistently rapid delivery. In these situations, the sales force are primarily involved in sophisticated quality discussions – unit cost takes a back seat to the broader JIT quality requirements.

Put simply, JIT is a system where stockholding is controlled and restricted so that it allows "pull" in the market by delivering input to production or distribution centers only at the rate and time it is needed. JIT enthusiasts contrast it with the older methods that were "just in case," in the sense that firms tried to cope with fluctuating demand by holding large amounts of stock, which tied up capital and reduced profitability. Developments in IT have helped JIT to massively reduce working capital needs while maintaining or even improving delivery rates. JIT can be used solely within a firm, or along the distribution channel of several firms.

In Japan, the "Kanban" JIT system works by rapidly passing information up and down the supply chain. Retailers pass back details of firm and tentative orders from their customers, enabling, for example, car manufacturers to make individual products to order with extraordinarily short lead times (10 days is typical). Clearly, such perfect efficiency implies very close cooperation between firms, which may never become possible in the short-termist, stock-market-driven Western economies. It also requires buying in many components rather than manufacturing them internally, thus extending the required chain of cooperation and requiring all suppliers to be closely involved from the design stage onward. The sales force become a liaison between firms ensuring that crucial information is transmitted and understood. There is little room for error, but JIT supporters argue that this pressure actually leads to improved products as everyone is focused on getting it right first time.

JIT cannot be established quickly. Toyota took two decades to develop a satisfactory system. Critics point out that political and regulatory changes and labor problems can severely disrupt JIT, hence Japanese firms' insistence on making single union deals when they set up their manufacturing plants in Britain. The extreme discipline of JIT looks risky to many firms, but the competitive advantages of being able to produce high-quality products very rapidly with almost no waste are forcing companies in mature or commodity industries, such as car manufacturing, to adopt some form of this approach.

As with KAM, in relationship selling costs may become transparent; both companies know the costs and prices of the other's goods precisely and agree upon profit margins in advance. This arrangement, known as "open accounting," means that salespeople do not subsequently discuss pricing at all.

The main goal of relationship selling is to retain the customer. For the individual salesperson, life can be relatively sedate, calling only on regular customers, enjoying job security and a clearly defined career path, and being paid a salary plus annual bonuses rather than commissions per sale.

In the PC industry, some major manufacturers are using working groups to control their buying. For example, IBM has a Strategic Equipment Council and Intel has a Process Equipment Development Committee to evaluate potential suppliers and recommend purchasing policies. For the supplier, such groups present special challenges. Often more than one group is involved in the decision-making process, and the supplier needs to discover the dynamics of the process as early as possible. By building an organization chart of the customer's committees that maps both the formal and informal lines of authority, the supplier can plan its strategy with precision. The supplier must find out what the objectives of each group are, if there are key individuals who can reverse the collective decisions, and whether there are any issues upon which there is already a consensus of opinion. It is also vital to learn if there are any committed supporters or enemies of your competitors in these groups, and how your firm is viewed in comparison to the competition.

In such situations, the selling process becomes something of a poker game. Considerable detective work is needed before making any serious presentation to the group. Often the selling process can take years, and suppliers need to find committee members who will help to coach them through the process. A "nice guy" coach can be dangerous, since he or she may fold under pressure at internal meetings, while strongly outspoken people may appear to wield more influence than is actually the case. Sometimes, a quiet technician who is not a member of the group can have a powerful effect by producing reports that support your product – the very fact that he or she is only concerned with technical matters may give such reports greater weight.

SALES RECRUITMENT

The sales force generally suffer from a high turnover of staff and a wide variation in performance. In a 1979 British study by PA Consultants for the Institute of Marketing, for example, most sales managers said they would expect a substantial increase in sales (over 16%) within two years if they assigned their best salesperson to the territory of an average salesperson and made no other changes; 20% of respondents said they would expect an increase of 30% or more. Since salespeople are expensive, firms are interested in ways of either only selecting the best potential performers or else training all recruits to become high achievers, but the consensus is that no amount of training and motivational work can be an adequate substitute for certain innate individual qualities (see Chapter 8, "What makes a good salesperson?").

Many people are attracted to sales, but surveys repeatedly find that as few as 30% of new recruits ever become satisfactory performers in the long term. For the trainee, a career in sales sadly remains very much "sink or swim."

Writing a clear job description is the first step in recruitment. Usually prepared by the sales manager, the job description should cover:

» The job title.
» The duties and responsibilities – the products, markets and customers, the selling tasks, after-sales service, and information feedback.
» Technical knowledge – how deeply the salesperson needs to understand the product.
» Location – where the salesperson will work.
» Degree of autonomy.

These definitions serve to narrow down potential applicants, but care is needed not to exclude promising people, for example because of lack of experience.

There are various sources of applicants. The main ones are:

» Within the company – the advantage is that applicants will be well known to the company, although they will be coming from a non-sales background.
» Educational institutions – students of business may be intelligent and have up-to-date technical training. They may see a sales job just as a step on the road to a managerial position, however, and perform poorly when they discover that selling is not easy.
» Competing firms – "poaching" upsets the competition but is attractive because applicants already know their business well. Recruiters need to be careful not to employ the "dogs" that other firms are eager to see the back of.

» Other industries – applicants may have good sales experience, but will need to adapt to the new business and may require extensive training to unlearn old habits.

» The unemployed – training and careful screening are necessary.

» Recruitment agencies – this is a costly method, and critics argue that the best salespeople have no need of agencies. Approach with caution.

Sometimes new recruits are found through personal contacts, but usually the firm will advertise. Ads in the national press on days that have recruitment features are seen to be effective in Britain. Local press and trade journals are also worthwhile.

RESEARCHING YOUR POTENTIAL EMPLOYERS

Professional investors rarely risk their money on a firm without performing a "due diligence" investigation, so why should salespeople risk their "human capital" (time) by taking a job with the wrong company? One way to gather reliable information about a potential employer is the "scuttlebutt" networking technique defined by the highly successful investor Philip Fisher.

In his book, *Common Stocks and Uncommon Profits* (Wiley, 1996), Fisher writes: "Most people love to talk about their competitors. Go to key managers in five different companies in an industry and ask each of them questions about the other four. You will emerge with a detailed and accurate picture of all five companies!" As well as competitors, other sources worth approaching are suppliers, customers, former employees, and trade association staff.

The direct approach may be unwise since it may make people feel uncomfortable and reluctant to give full answers. It is more effective to start a discussion about the industry as a whole, interleaving questions about your target firm. Many people feel more comfortable talking in comparative terms about the various competitors in a market; you can learn much unpublished information about a company's growth prospects, methods, products, and policies in this way.

Here's a checklist of important points to research.

» Products – do the firm's products and services have a good potential for sales growth over the medium term?

» The sales force – a firm's customers will have much valuable knowledge about the effectiveness of its salespeople. Are they effective? What is the after-sales service like? Are they responsive to customer needs? How are they managed?

» Profits and prices – how do they compare with the competition?

» Is it a nice company? Many people in an industry will have a good idea about how a firm treats its employees; is it a good firm to work for, or does it "use and abuse" its people before sacking them for a fresh batch?

» Quality of management – is the company well run and on top of its game? Do senior executives have integrity? Are sales managers fair-minded and effective?

"Scuttlebutt" will never give you comprehensive information, but it is likely that a firm's major flaws and advantages will emerge as you cross-reference the various opinions of the people you talk to. In the case of start-ups, where the company does not have a track record, informal detective work about the founders is even more vital.

KEY LEARNING POINTS

» Centralized buying, consolidation in high-tech industries, and the general globalization trend are leading many firms to concentrate their efforts on complex sales to a few larger customers, the "key accounts." Salespeople are focused on quality issues rather than cost, and some firms even operate "open accounting" where their exact profit margins are known and pre-agreed by the customer.

» "Reverse marketing," where the buyer aggressively seeks out suppliers, is becoming more common, but in some industries sellers are reluctant to enter into long-term key account relationships because of the buyer's power. In the semiconductor field, for example, the industry is dominated by manufacturers who make heavy demands of their suppliers. The upside is massive sales potential and the kudos of selling to a major name, but the risks are high, particularly for small, vulnerable firms.

» Just-in-time (JIT) systems, originally from Japan, attempt to eliminate waste and drastically reduce inventory by delivering parts and finished products exactly when needed along the supply chain. While successful JIT is extremely efficient, it presupposes excellent industrial relations and a stable business environment. Even a small hiccup can cause the whole system to collapse, and there is doubt over whether "pure" JIT can ever become widespread outside Japan.

» Key account management and relationship selling require a very different kind of salesperson to the traditional maverick working alone out in the field, offering a more sedate working life as part of a highly coordinated team.

» Sales force turnover is generally very high in most industries, but no sure-fire solution for eliminating this problem has yet been identified. For companies, as well as the individuals concerned, this is unsatisfactory because of the high costs involved. Applicants for sales positions would do well to investigate their potential employers thoroughly, in particular by approaching others in the industry for their views on the company. For the individual, the "human capital" of time invested in working for a firm is at least as valuable as a financial investment, so it is important to make sure that your employers are people worth working for!

In Practice – Sales Success Stories

» Network marketing: Amway
» The changing face of Japanese car selling
» Sotheby's: adding value through sales skills.

NETWORK MARKETING: AMWAY

Imagine selling household detergents or vitamins on a national scale in the United States without advertising your brand at all. Imagine having your distributors pay for all your marketing. Imagine a huge and enthusiastic sales force that work on rather low commission with no salary.

Imagine all of these and you imagine Amway in its glory, before the Internet, the greatest network of all, started to chomp away at the greatest network marketing company in the world.

There are probably more sites pointing out the supposed evils of Amway than against any other major US corporation. But it is perfectly legal, say the courts, and Alticor and Quixstar, as Amway is now called, have scaled US business into a $7 billion global company.

A future historian of sales strategies might write a dissertation on the particular Amway genius of industrializing the intimacy of personal networks of friends into direct sales of the most mundane consumer goods. Without doubt, Amway thrived because it realized from the very start that, as in most sales activities, more benefits are on the table than meet the eye. In most consumer goods the extra, non-product factors are psychological and almost inevitably focused on inculcating feelings the potential consumer might want to have about him- or herself. "If I buy shampoo X I will look better and younger." "If I buy detergent Y then I will be fulfilling by duty to my family by giving them really clean sheets that smell of fresh flowers." "If I buy Vodka Z I will be one of those wealthy, sophisticated, and knowledgeable people who look as if they are always on TV and have many lovers."

One of the reasons for Amway's amazing sales success was that it actually went beyond the norms and delivered on the subliminal or explicit promises made to its customers. Besides household cleaning products, vitamins, water purifiers, or cosmetics it was selling belonging, optimism, tools for success, and a supposedly wide-open meritocracy. It delivered on these promises in endless conferences, meetings, motivational tapes, and the ubiquitous Amvox voicemail service that glued the whole operation together.

Amway worked as follows. Every person who was a potential customer was also invited to be a distributor. They would buy several hundred dollars' worth of goods, and then invest somewhere between $1000 and £2000 a year in various seller kits and other materials. It was not a pyramid scheme, the courts ruled, because there were real goods making their way to real kitchen sinks. Now the way to make, say, 100 dollars' worth of goods even cheaper was to persuade other people to buy them. For that, however, one had to be a distributor. Using highly complicated formulas, each distributor got a certain percentage of the sales below him or her on the ladder. Those quite far up – or upline as they are called in Amway parlance – did make a fair amount of money. The more they flaunted this money at the various, almost evangelical Amway conventions of distributors, the more they created incentives for those further down the line to try to rope in more distributors.

The margins on these goods for Amway were highly satisfactory because there was none of the huge marketing and advertising expense associated with competing consumer goods in the US market. This meant that the company could tolerate a fairly high drop-out rate of potential distributors. Repeated challenges in court created a situation in which the Amway Multi Level Marketing formula was effectively regulated by legal precedent that determined that the company had to:

» demand that its distributors create part of their business in real sales of products rather than in just enlisting new members to the scheme; and

» state very clearly to new members (in the United States) that the average earnings of an Amway distributor were considerably less than $100 a month.

These limitations did not stop Amway's growth, which proves either that suckers never die because they are just replaced by others, or – alternatively – that the other non-tangible goods purveyed by the Amway network were in fact fulfilling the stated and less stated desires of members of the network. In terms of sales management one of the most brilliant aspects of multi-level marketing of this kind is that the core corporation, by definition, does not pay the cost of inefficiency. All the costs associated with sales inefficiency are pushed out to the network and the costs of sales is always clear and predictable.

As in any organization, the sales results depend largely on the degree of enthusiasm and creativity displayed by line salespeople balanced by the level of management controls and strategic guidance that tie in these individual efforts. But unlike other organizations, Amway found ways in which the costs of motivating and controlling the line salespeople were borne by members of the network.

The payoff, for people fairly high up the network, was that Amway allowed them to conduct in effect a separate line of business along the same sales and communication channels. This business dealt largely with motivational tapes, brochures, and other materials sold at a fairly high cost by people high up the network to those further down. Structurally, this separate line of business ensured that those high up in the network had an immediate and pressing interest to be in constant touch with those further down. Psychologically, the tapes and other material filled a role in outlining the non-product aspirations of the low-level distributors.

As a multi-level marketer, Amway, throughout its history, faced constant criticism, investigations, and legal threats from people or organizations who were disenchanted with its methods of selling and recruiting new distributors. Putting the ethical questions aside (is it more ethical to promise a woman that she will look young and beautiful by using a certain face cream or to promise her that she will be rich if she sells detergents?), there are interesting questions of sales force structure in the Amway scheme of affairs – questions that became all the more relevant in 2001–2 when the US sales of Amway and its associated Quixstar corporation declined.

Amway is based on a classical hierarchical structure somewhat analogous to feudalism under a strong king who ensures that everybody marches to the same drum. Distributors, or salespeople, are recruited individually, by individuals. Those higher up the system are given names like emeralds, diamonds, or double diamonds. They earn money directly from sales of their own promotional material and from sales of Amway products from those further down. All of this happens within a complex set of rules and regulations which, quite naturally, are better known to those higher up in the system. Tying the whole system together is a complex communications and distribution system paid for by members of the network.

Now what happens when a classic top-down structure meets something as structurally anarchic as, say, the Internet? It does not work too well – even on a simple information level. Let's imagine potential Amway distributors in a small town in the Midwest during the 1970s. If they had any questions about Amway, their best way of getting answers would be to talk to people in the network, preferably those higher up with more experience. Today that same person would immediately go online where they would find literally hundreds of Websites devoted to denigrating Amway (whether for better or worse reasons). The second step that hypothetical new distributor might make would be to go to Ebay and check out the price of vitamins of the kind sold by Amway. That second step is literally lethal for companies like Amway.

Probably realizing this problem, Quixstar was launched by the owner of Amway to try to move the operation online. Unofficial reports (the company is privately held) show that the results have been less than completely satisfactory even though they are obscured by the fact that so much of Amway's business is now under the Quixstar name. The Quixstar promise is similar to Amway's: be independent and run your own shop.

The complicated system of up- and downline compensation on the hybrid Amway Quixstar business in 2001 pointed to a new reality. First of all, the network was offering non-Amway products – in response to the pressures of the wide open world the Net created. But these brand-name products in the US market were obviously less lucrative since consumers would have to pay the costs of advertising and marketing – and also had the opportunity to do comparison shopping in Wal-Mart.

One need not be too concerned for the Amway concept. It was born in the United States where management spent 40 years honing the sales and distribution system. It is still a moot question of how it will overcome the double challenge of the Internet to its hierarchical system. But the system is a fundamentally innovative sales management scheme, and as such shows signs of doing very well in less sophisticated countries wherever it lands, be it China or Eastern Europe.

THE CHANGING FACE OF JAPANESE CAR SELLING

Once upon a time there was a myth that Japanese business practices were so incredibly superior they were bound to take over the world. Two or three myths later (remember the one about Internet traffic being more important than profits?) the conventional wisdom around

2002 was that domestic Japanese business was so hopelessly stagnant there was not a chance it could ever recover. That too could be wrong.

Car dealerships were often used as an example of a good sales technique that had become hopelessly inefficient in Japan. Where else in the world, it was argued, do salespeople sell cars door to door and visit the customer at home *after* the car was actually sold to ask how he or she felt about the new car? And where else could you go to, say, a Toyota dealership and be told that only certain kinds of passenger cars made by Toyota were available in this area?

The classic Japanese car sales network consists of dealerships that specialize in certain parts of the manufacturer's line deemed suitable for the neighborhood or region. The manufacturers also protect the dealers from infringements on their territory by rival dealerships; effectively creating fiefs for the dealership that in return had to match up to rigorously defined sales quotas.

Salespeople would ring doorbells without prior appointments and get to know hundreds of people, all of whom were potential customers. They would chat, see how things were going, and then maybe come again for a few times until they got down to business. This enabled them to:

» really get to know their customers;
» know when a potential customer could be persuaded to buy a new car; and
» have a good idea of what kind of car each person could afford after seeing their home and getting a feeling for their income level and lifestyle.

This method was reinforced by several extraneous factors. The first is a highly expensive and demanding system for testing used vehicles called the "shaken." This system makes it hardly worthwhile to keep any car for more than seven to nine years because the cost of getting the necessary vehicular approval and compulsory insurance tended to rise over the years. The system is so demanding that it created a major industry of exporting perfectly good used Japanese cars all over the world. The second was financial arrangements that traditionally allowed customers who traded-in their cars to complete the purchase with very low down payments at highly advantageous interest rates. The third was cultural, with a traditionally strong bias toward owning new vehicles. For many people, owning a used car is shameful and something they would rather hide.

This was the classic picture true for most of the 1990s. Toyota, for example, maintained five separate chains of sales channels in Japan, each with somewhere between 650 and 1300 new car outlets. These chains were originally set up according to rigorous consumer profiling. But Japan was changing and by the late 1990s at least one of the sales channels was based on showrooms as in the United States and not on home visits.

There was nothing intrinsically wrong with this highly complicated and well-managed system. (Indeed, dealers of more expensive cars in the United States are thinking of adopting the Japanese home visit techniques to suit what they think are the real needs of a more affluent customer base.) But what clearly had changed was the access to information, and the desire to shop for better prices.

Research shows that Japanese car customers are fairly satisfied with their traditional dealers but fed up with the lack of variety in the preordained choices of their neighborhood dealership. They quite simply want to buy at dealerships with a complete product range and preferably from dealers representing more than one manufacturer. All over the world it seems people in the market for, say, a minivan would prefer to go to a minivan dealer who has models from various manufacturers. That is the last thing that Japanese manufacturers would want, but the market might well evolve in that direction because the first mover would have a tremendous advantage.

But in the meantime, until that happens, the availability of comprehensive pricing information has allowed Japanese customers, like those all over the world, to demand that their neighborhood dealer match the prices presented in deep-discount sites online.

Despite their unhappiness with the traditional way of affairs, Japanese consumers did not fall for the US alternative to the sleazy car dealership – the Saturn concept with its no-frills, no-bargain approach to everything. Saturn closed down its Japanese dealerships apparently because the Japanese consumer still wanted the personal attention that the classic dealership and salesmen allowed.

The biggest news in the Japanese auto industry is that it is doing very well in terms of domestic sales because it is changing the most important element of the mix – the cars. The tremendous changes taking place in Japanese society are beyond the scope of this chapter, but it is enough to say that the young urban sophisticates of Tokyo no longer have either the job security that their parents had or the desire to buy the bland sedans coming out of Japan during the past 10 years.

Toyota started to experiment with a car designed specifically for women, with color-coordinated hubcaps and a rounded look that focus groups found attractive. It took off well but languished after a while. It was followed by models with names like bB WiLL VS or Vitz and looks that go far beyond the traditional Japanese family car.

Toyota is bringing these cars to market in its Vista dealership and is selling them mostly in showrooms. Another sales channel called Netz is targeted specifically at entry-level cars for the important youth market. The focus is also moving away from homes. Some Netz dealerships, for example, have on-site pizza parlors and places for kids to play while their parents look at the trendy new cars. Instead of relaxing at home while hearing the pitch one could relax at the dealership – or so the thinking might go.

All of these revolutions in the years 2001 and 2002 were happening at a time of unprecedented change for the Japanese auto industry. When ordinary Japanese people started admiring the Brazilian-born Carlos Ghosn for the way he was revolutionizing Nissan – with massive layoffs – the door was opened to changing sales techniques and channels.

Not everybody is a twenty-something Tokyo graduate with orange hair and an ultra cool attitude, and more boring cars are still sold to ordinary Japanese consumers who appreciate the care, attention, and personal interaction of the old way of buying cars. So what seems to be developing is an interesting hybrid that preserves harmony among the various players in the market – an important consideration in Japan – while allowing radical change to take place.

As more shopping, and especially price research, goes online, the major players in the online auto sales market are giving consumers all the information, options, and alternatives they want, and then sending them to the neighborhood dealer to actually close the deal. This preserves the dealership and that level of personal attention that Japanese consumers really want. These consumers, it turns out, want more variety and better process but are very happy with the copious amounts of information they are getting from the old-fashioned salesman.

Showrooms and dealerships have started to push their inventory to another category of online dealers who are discounting these cars and selling them without any of the special care and attention customers get for the premium price. This in effect releases a lot of pressure on the system because it creates a no-frills baseline for those customers who want it that way. But in a country where the art of wrapping reaches such incredible heights not everybody wants a no-frill car purchase.

There was nothing really wrong with the traditional Japanese car sales model. In fact, it was a brilliant way of keeping loyal customers and pushing to buy the latest new car. It depended, however, on several factors like:

» lack of competitive pricing information;
» the ability to maintain clearly defined territories between dealerships; and
» a social structure based on families who mostly buy sedans or small SUVs.

But as Japan is changing with smaller families and less security the sales model has to evolve too. The industry has shown that it knows that it has to do more than re-engineer sales channels. It is a complex process that starts with a better, broader product mix, gives consumers more choices from within the manufacturer's line, allows for integration of on- and offline purchases, and yet maintains that crucial and highly valuable personal contact that made the Japanese auto industry so strong in the first place.

SOTHEBY'S: ADDING VALUE THROUGH SALES SKILLS

The psychologist Maslow's classic theory of the hierarchy of needs, developed in the 1940s (see Chapter 3), has become something of a cliché in marketing textbooks, and often seems to have little relevance in the modern world where, in the affluent West at least, physical needs (the most pressing, according to Maslow) are amply provided for most people and the very "post-modern" troubles of psychological alienation and lack of meaning seem to fit awkwardly into the theory. In the case of the art world, however, Maslow's ideas seem to fit very well. Nobody "needs" art, yet during good times some of the rich are willing to pay colossal sums for paintings and other antique treasures, largely out of what Maslow defined as "social needs" – the need to belong to an in-group and the desire for prestige and high perceived status.

During the latter half of the twentieth century, fine art auctioneering became big business, finding ways of exploiting the curious psychology of an expanding market. Although transactions between fading aristocracy and the newly rich have always been common – marriage between a titled pauper and a commercial heiress was a common theme in nineteenth-century fiction, for example – Sotheby's and its arch-rival Christie's discovered ways of creating legions of completely new buyers.

Successful fine art auctioneering is a supreme selling job, and much depends upon the image of the auctioneer. In the eighteenth century, Christie's founder, James Christie, was the first to make attending fine art auctions fashionable in a London that was prospering wildly from the fruits of the Industrial Revolution. A man of great charm, his contemporaries reported that ladies would say he was irresistible. One of Christie's great achievements was to remove any social reluctance to sell; even royalty would sell jewelry and pictures through him, and business boomed after the French Revolution of 1789 as distressed French aristocrats sought to raise cash from what treasures they had managed to remove from France. He even auctioned the jewelry of Madame du Barry, Louis XV's mistress, after her execution in 1793.

Sotheby's was established at about the same time as Christie's, but had specialized in book auctions, a less glamorous trade that relied on scholarship and integrity rather than razzamatazz. When new partners took over in 1909, the firm began to be more entrepreneurial. One area that it expanded into was discreet private sales, where embarrassed vendors did not want their need for cash publicized; these tended to yield a much greater commission than the 12.5% they received from auctions. Sotheby's managed to sell a collection of early books, including 13 printed by Caxton, to US tycoon J. Pierpont Morgan for nearly $20 million in today's money, and another sale of volumes belonging to the Duke of Devonshire netted a similar amount, going to H.E. Huntington, an American railroad magnate. The commissions on these two sales alone were the equivalent of several years' profits, and the firm was now in a different league. In 1913 it auctioned chattels from the estate of the poet Robert Browning, including the controversial love letters he wrote to Elizabeth Barrett, with whom he had scandalously eloped. Through careful scholarship Sotheby's was able to produce a catalog that shed new light on the scandal, allowing the public to enjoy the voyeuristic excitement of the sale with a serious-minded alibi. This was a formula which was to prove very lucrative in the future. The sale attracted enormous publicity and was heavily reported in the national press. Although the letters went to one of the usual dealers, the media exposure helped to foster the elite image of the auctioneer – you knew you had arrived socially, when you buy and sell at Sotheby's.

For many years Christie's and Sotheby's had had an understanding not to poach on each other's territories – Christie's sold pictures and Sotheby's sold books. Not long after the Browning coup, Sotheby's made a bold move that changed this relationship for ever, by offering a painting by the Dutch master Frans Hals. By chance, Christie's was also selling two Frans Hals paintings on the same day, but Sotheby's picture sold for the most that any painting fetched that year, a direct result of the public attention that Sotheby's was enjoying. From then on, the two auctioneers became fierce rivals.

Just after the end of World War I, Sotheby's moved to new premises in fashionable Mayfair and began to compete aggressively for business, cutting its commission from 12.5% to 7.5% on pictures, jewelry, furniture, and other categories in which Christie's had the greater market share. The firm cultivated journalists, encouraging them to write up the auctions in as glamorous terms as possible.

World War I was the catalyst for radical social change. Aristocrats had lost their power, and were suffering from heavy new taxes designed to redistribute wealth. A flood of treasures came on the market, going principally to foreign buyers such as the many new museums springing up in America.

Traditionally, the very finest pieces were never offered at auction, but went through an elite group of dealers. Sotheby's was approached by a distinguished scholar, Charles Bell, of the Ashmolean Museum at

Oxford, to sell an inherited collection of drawings. Bell had written his own catalog, which was of a much higher intellectual standard than anything any auctioneer had ever produced, and the sale went well.

Bell became a regular cataloger for the fine art auctions, but refused to succumb to the commercial pressure to hype goods. In one sale of Old Master drawings, for example, Bell's catalog did not identify any one of the 14 Rembrandts as being certainly by the master, but qualified them as "school of," "manner of," or other cautious definitions. Bell's reluctance to attribute unless he was absolutely sure was an enormous boost to Sotheby's image. Bell's catalogs had scholarly integrity, and if he said that a painting was definitely by a certain artist, people believed him. Better paintings began to arrive at Sotheby's door and by 1927 the two rival auctioneers were enjoying a roughly equal share of the market. In need of new capital, Sotheby's brought more partners into the business.

Sotheby's began to move in on another of Christie's preserves, the grand country house sale, using a "Flying Squad" that read the obituary columns and scoured the countryside looking for business. The biggest coup was in 1937 when the Rothschild family sold the contents of their Piccadilly mansion; BBC radio broadcast live coverage of the sale, and buyers queued for hours to get in.

World War II brought a flood of talented refugees from the continental art world to England, but most of the treasures went to America where they could fetch better prices. After the war business was slow in the newly impoverished Britain, and the firm sought to internationalize its business. In 1952 the King of Egypt was deposed by a military coup, and Sotheby's began negotiating for the right to sell the monarch's vast collections, including an impressive hoard of erotica. Persuading the new Egyptian government to pass a law confiscating the property, Sotheby's won the lion's share of the sale, which was held in Cairo in a blaze of international publicity.

In 1956 the firm seized upon a chance to break the top dealers' stranglehold on the best Old Master paintings when it discovered a Poussin that had been forgotten for more than a century. Dealers got wind of the deal and tried to purchase the picture from its English owner, forcing Sotheby's to secretly guarantee a very high price for the picture. The picture sold for £6000 less than the guarantee and the firm had to make up the difference, but the sale was hailed by the art world as a triumph. Believing that they would make more money from an auction than a private sale, owners of great paintings started to come in, and prices began to break records.

Auctioneers' commissions were much higher in the United States, and by the late 1950s American-owned treasures were being shipped to London to be sold, ironically, mainly to American buyers. A few years later, the two rivals both set up shop in New York, with Sotheby's buying the New York auctioneer Parke Bernet.

The postwar boom encouraged more and more countries to set up museums, and every museum had to have its prestige pieces. By the early 1960s, Sotheby's realized that the supply of Old Masters would eventually dry up, since museums are unlikely ever to sell their best treasures. New categories of painting were hyped, such as works by Stubbs and Canaletto, while Sotheby's sought fresh goods as diverse as photographs (the first sale took place in 1967) and vintage cars. By the 1970s, it was possible to achieve high prices for modern art by painters such as Andy Warhol, and Sotheby's also expanded into real estate agency, selling millionaire homes in the United States to celebrities, a very profitable art education program, wine, jewelry, movie props, and the personal possessions of famous people; in 1996, a sale of nearly 6000 items belonging to Jacqueline Kennedy Onassis, including cigarette lighters, stools, and golf clubs, fetched fabulous prices despite the fact that they had little intrinsic value. Sotheby's had discovered a way of supplying the huge demand for possessing a little bit of fame and glamor that went far beyond the aesthetic tastes of the traditional art world.

Both Christie's and Sotheby's are publicly listed companies now, which has somewhat cramped the style of their traditionally anarchic business methods, but both firms continue to do what they do best: find beautiful or "famous" things and hype the buyers into a frenzy.

KEY INSIGHTS

Managing a sales force is a costly business, and many firms have moved out of personal selling to focus on channels with lower overheads. Network marketing, as practiced by Amway, sought a different solution: why not persuade naive consumers to do all the selling, direct to their neighbors? By devolving most of the costs of selling on the "distributors" and providing a gung-ho support system, Amway made money in the United States for itself and the "upline" distributors, although most people involved made less than $100 a month. The advent of the Internet, allowing consumers to compare prices more easily, seems to have hurt Amway's growth in the United States, but it is now actively expanding into less developed markets such as Eastern Europe, China, and Southeast Asia. It remains to be seen how long the scheme can last.

Japan's uniquely hierarchical culture enabled car manufacturers to employ selling methods that would not work anywhere else, namely selling door to door. Japanese society is changing, however, and the traditional system is losing ground a little, in particular because consumers are demanding more choice. Personal service is desired, however, and people would rather get close attention than a lower price – a happy situation for personal sellers!

Not many companies have survived for 250 years. Sotheby's and its rival Christie's have done so by the consummate skill with which they serve the market for prestige art and collectibles. Two keys to their continuing success have been their profound understanding of their customers' psychology and their ability to generate enormous publicity around a major sale. The antics of the very rich always makes good copy, and the auctioneers have been able to expand into less moneyed markets as a result; there are many good works of art that are nevertheless not the "best," but are still highly desired by the middle classes. By using every selling tactic available, from harnessing the skills of academics to exploiting the expansionist activities of museums, the two firms look set to survive and prosper for many years to come.

Key Concepts and Thinkers

» What makes a good salesperson?
» Psychological tests
» Personality testing – the Minnesota Multiphasic Personality Inventory (MMPI)
» Staying motivated
» Closing techniques
» Glossary.

WHAT MAKES A GOOD SALESPERSON?

In 1964 two respected researchers, David Mayer and Herbert Greenberg, published a brief article in the *Harvard Business Review* entitled "What makes a good salesman?" Based on the results of a seven-year study that examined why there was a high turnover in US sales staff, Mayer and Greenberg argued that personal characteristics, specifically "empathy" and "ego drive," were more important for success than sales experience, and that sales training was not likely to be successful if the wrong people were recruited. They saw the effective salesperson as one who

> senses the reactions of the customer and is able to adjust to these reactions. He is not simply bound by a prepared sales track, but he functions in terms of real interaction between himself and the customer. Sensing what the customer is feeling, he is able to change pace, double back on his track, and make whatever creative modifications might be necessary to home in on the target and close the sale.

Mayer and Greenberg maintained that only two qualities were essential to success at selling: "empathy" and "ego drive." They defined "empathy" as the ability to put oneself in the buyer's place and understand his or her needs and problems, and "ego drive" as a desire to make the sale over and above the wish to make money. Using a psychological test, the MMPI (see below), they found a good correlation between a high score in these characteristics and sales success in the insurance, car, and mutual fund industries.

After initial failures to attract corporate interest, Mayer and Greenberg were about to close their business down when General Motors asked them to test the sales force of their worst-performing division, Buick. Following this break, their approach rapidly gained wide acceptance, first in the auto industry and then across corporate America.

Today, Herbert Greenberg is CEO of Caliper, a firm that "measures the innate abilities" of job candidates, with more than 20,000 corporate clients including Merrill Lynch and Avis. Says Greenberg,

The American mentality, the apple-pie mentality, is, "By God, if you work hard enough, you can succeed at anything!" There's 10 percent truth to that; you can make yourself survive in a job and not get fired. But you can't really fly in the face of who you are as a person and succeed at a high level.

Greenberg has been fighting a 40-year battle against the view that a manager can pick the right candidate by intuition: "Back then, you'd hear, 'I can recognize somebody! I just look them in the eye and I can tell right away if they want to work or not!'"

PSYCHOLOGICAL TESTS

Recruiting the wrong staff is costly, especially for large organizations, so some firms use psychological tests as an aid to identifying candidates with good potential. Such tests are useless in untrained hands, and can even be damaging, so it is essential to hire trained clinical psychologists to conduct and analyze them. This means that testing is not cheap; the cost per individual tested can be thousands of dollars.

Tests rarely give unambiguous results; for example, it is possible for candidates to "cheat" by answering in a way that presents them in the best light. Some tests measure the interests of candidates, but this may not be effective, since candidates with similar interests to top-performing salespeople are not necessarily top performers themselves. Furthermore, selecting people who have desirable characteristics for sales work, such as sociability, loyalty, and dominance, may not discriminate between good and bad performers.

Careless use of tests can lead to litigation; in the early 1990s, a job seeker sued an employer, Target, on the grounds that the firm had invaded the candidate's privacy by asking him to take the Minnesota Multiphasic Personality Inventory test. The California court granted a preliminary injunction against the use of the test in hiring, but the case was eventually settled out of court. Firms are within their rights to administer such tests, but in the United States they may be sued on the grounds of invasion of privacy or sexual/racial discrimination.

Despite the problems, the need to recruit good salespeople who stay with the firm is driving many companies to use psychological tests.

Popular tests include the Predictive Index, the Myers–Briggs Personality Indicator, the Personal Profile System, and the Minnesota Multiphasic Personality Inventory.

PERSONALITY TESTING – THE MINNESOTA MULTIPHASIC PERSONALITY INVENTORY (MMPI)

The Minnesota Multiphasic Personality Inventory, or MMPI, was developed in the late 1930s by a psychologist and a psychiatrist at the University of Minnesota, and was substantially revised in 1989 as the MMPI-2. Much used in court cases in the United States, the MMPI is widely regarded as one of the most effective ways of measuring personality if properly conducted, being very well researched and easy to administer.

It has a number of scales which were originally meant to measure "pure" psychiatric disorders, with dramatic names such as the "hypochondriasis" scale and the "schizophrenia" scale. Subsequent research showed that these scales were not good measures of "pure" mental disorders – for instance, a high score on the schizophrenia scale did not necessarily mean that you were schizophrenic – so they are now more often referred to by number ("Scale 1," "Scale 2," and so on). People commonly produce high scores on more than one scale, and it has been found that it is possible to build a reliable personality "profile" based on the interpretation of scores on several scales in combination.

Like most personality tests, it is possible to "fake" the test by giving answers intended to present a particular impression. The MMPI has several "validity" scales designed to detect faking and inconsistency – for example, someone who claims never to have lied in their entire lifetime is likely to be faking, and someone who says that "most of the time I feel blue" and later that "I am happy most of the time" may simply be responding randomly. The validity tests are quite effective, but the well-informed faker may be able to defeat them.

Taking and processing the MMPI is time consuming – it contains hundreds of questions – and there are computer programs that collate the answers and generate the various scales in graphical form. While this makes large-scale testing easier, it has also made the test easy to misuse. Most programs use MMPI "cookbooks" of standard interpretations to generate a psychological profile but which fail to take the individual's circumstances (environment, life experiences, and current difficulties) into account. These standardized interpretations have a spurious air of authority, and can be used by unqualified people to draw inaccurate conclusions about the person being tested.

For this reason, the MMPI test should only be used by a clinical psychologist; even a professional psychiatrist or social worker is unlikely to be competent enough to interpret the results appropriately.

The psychologist needs to know about the background of the person being tested and must integrate the test results with other information before making a judgment based on his or her psychological knowledge. As an aid to recruitment it is a powerful tool, but is probably only cost effective for large organizations who can afford the time and expense. To validate the test, the MMPI is given to existing sales staff whose performance records are known; this provides benchmarks for the various selling roles within the firm. The profiles of candidates can then be compared to the benchmarks to identify individuals who are likely to perform well. Over time, the benchmarks can be further refined by analyzing how closely the performance of new recruits matched the original predictions.

STAYING MOTIVATED

Salespeople are the front line troops in a company. They must face rejection and conflict on a daily basis, and constantly struggle to maintain a high level of positive emotional energy. It is small wonder that maintaining strong motivation is a problem, and that even experienced salespeople suffer from periods of depression, or seek to avoid challenging situations by, for example, only calling on established clients. The fear of going out on the road day after day can lead many salespeople to find any excuse to hang around the office as much as possible, trying to look busy. While the best salespeople find their own personal ways to stay positive, companies find they have to provide motivation, especially for their average and poor performers. Meetings, conferences, prizes, parties, and training are all used as ways of keeping up the morale of the sales force, often to little effect.

The fact is that staying motivated and coping with constant rejection is an emotional challenge rather than an intellectual one. Apparently juvenile activities, such as reciting affirmations or holding group bull sessions, can provide the morale boosts that salespeople need to stay positive. Non-salespeople often unfairly mock the appetite that so many personal sellers have for pop psychology, motivational speakers, and so on – your favorite guru may be a phoney, but if his or her meetings and messages keep you positive and making calls, who cares?

CLOSING TECHNIQUES

As salespeople become more skilled, they are able to use risky closing techniques that would be likely to fail in the hands of a neophyte. But why try new techniques? The main reason is to increase the rate of success. Different personality types respond differently to a given approach, and there also are many situations where the customer is unlikely to buy without an inspired move on the part of the salesperson. Developing a wide repertoire of closing methods increases the seller's chances of making a sale.

Here's a brief look at some tried and tested "closes."

A basic industrial "close"

Most companies and public sector agencies only buy when they have assigned a purchase order (PO). Once the presentation has covered the customer's needs and how you can fulfil them, start asking for the PO number. The customers won't know it, but by getting them to obtain one during the presentation, you avoid leaving the meeting with a mere promise of a PO – any delay increases the chances of a lost sale.

Filling in the form

A skilled salesperson can push the client through the delicate transition between the presentation and the agreement to buy by starting to fill in the order form with the customer's requirements as he or she states them. If the customer points out that no decision has been made, you answer, "I know, I just want to make sure that we don't miss anything if you do decide to buy." By the time the presentation is finished, the order form may be almost completed, and it becomes psychologically easy for the customer to sign the agreement.

Pros and cons

Business customers may have difficulty in coming to a decision because of the complexity of the issues involved. One approach is to work through, on paper, the pros and cons of your product with them. On one side of the page you list all the benefits that the customer has agreed upon; then you invite the customer to list any objections, but without your help. It is likely that the number of benefits will be substantially greater than the number of objections. You count them aloud and suggest to the customer that his or her decision is now easy to make (buy the product!).

"I'll mull this over"

Customers frequently resist making a decision to buy by saying that they want time to think it over. In skilled hands, this apparently insurmountable block can be turned into an effective "close" because the customers have, in effect, run out of reasons not to buy. First, you agree with the customers' decision not to decide, and appear ready to leave. Then you ask the customers to confirm that they're thinking it over because they are seriously interested. They are likely to agree. After a few similar questions designed to make the customers say that the product meets their needs, you begin to probe by asking if the hesitation is because of various far-fetched reasons (doubts about the honesty of your firm, about the benefits you have already agreed upon, and so on). Each question is designed to elicit a "No, it's not because of that," thus reinforcing the customers' agreement to the benefit. This process often narrows the customers' hesitation down to the most common objection of all – a reluctance to part with money. If the customers admit that the real problem is the money, you then move in with your financial arguments – how the product only costs pennies a day, how it will increase productivity and profits, and so on.

Try before you buy

This risky technique is generally only appropriate for business sales. It depends upon:

» your company/sales manager having a high degree of faith in your selling abilities;
» a customer who really will benefit from the product and is nearly ready to buy, but baulks at the cost; and
» a genuinely superior product.

You offer the customer a free trial for a month. The customer accepts, because the product will make money during the period without any outlay. After a few days you call to check if the product is working well and if there are any problems, but you DO NOT attempt to close. At the end of the trial period, you hope to make the sale because the customer's staff have become so used to using the product that they don't want to lose it.

GLOSSARY

Account management – the ongoing strategic direction of major clients' business.

Benefits – those things that the service does for or means to buyers, rather than the factual descriptions of it (which are the features).

Closing – action taken to gain a commitment to buy or proceed onward toward the point where this can logically occur.

Cold calling – approaches by any method (face-to-face or telephone, say) to potential customers who have expressed no prior interest of any sort.

Competitor intelligence – the information collected about competitive products and services and their suppliers that may specifically be used to improve the approach taken on a call.

Country of origin – in most countries, a label must indicate where the product was made, and this may influence customers' perception of its quality.

Cross-selling – the selling technique of ensuring that a range of different services are bought from a client who starts by buying only one.

Ego drive/empathy – Mayer and Goldberg's terms for, respectively, the internal motivational drive that makes a good salesperson want to succeed, and the ability to see things from other peoples' (customers) point of view – and, importantly, being seen to do so.

Features – the factual things to be described about a service (see **Benefits**).

Field training – simply training, or development, activity away from any formal setting, undertaken out and about on territory.

Gatekeeper – someone who through their position can facilitate or deny access to a buyer (e.g. a secretary).

Handling objections – the stage of the sales presentation which is most highly interactive and where specific queries (or challenges) posed by potential buyers must be addressed to keep the positive side of the case in the majority.

Influencers – people who, while not having exclusive authority to buy, influence the buyer through, say, their recommendation.

Key/major/national accounts – a variety of names are used here. First, measures vary as to what a major customer is; simplistically it is only what an individual organization finds significant. A second significant factor is the lead time involved. In industries selling, say, capital equipment it may take many months from first meeting to contract and there is an overlap here with "major sales."

Need identification – the process of asking questions to discover what, exactly, clients want (and why) as a basis for deciding how to pitch the sales presentation.

Negotiation – a different, though closely allied, skill to selling and very important in some kinds of business (note: there is another ExpressExec volume, *Negotiating*, which can provide a useful reference).

On-the-job training – field training and development activity, often starting with joint calls with a manager.

Pie system – a structured way of managing the spread of customers and prospects around a sales territory.

Proposal – normally implies a written document, one including the price but more than a quotation – it spells out the case and most often reflects a clear brief which has been given or established.

Prospecting – the search for new contacts who may be potential clients; encompasses everything from cold calling to desk research to identify names.

Qualifying prospects – research or action to produce information to demonstrate that cold prospects are "warm".

Sales aids – anything used during the sales conversation to enhance what is said; may be items, information (say a graph), or even other people.

Sales audit – an occasional, systematic review of all aspects of the sales activity and its management to identify areas needing improvement, or working well and needing extension; a process that recognizes the inherent dynamic nature of sales.

Sales productivity – the sales equivalent of productivity in an area; the focus here is on efficiencies that maximize the amount of time spent with customers (rather than traveling, writing reports, etc.): it focuses on ratios and touches on anything that increases sales success, however measured.

Territory – the area covered by an individual salesperson; it is usually, but not always, geographic.

KEY LEARNING POINTS

- "Ego drive" (getting a sense of achievement from closing) and "empathy" (understanding the customer's point of view) may be the only essential characteristics that successful salespeople have in common.
- Don't be afraid of personality tests, but make sure that they are being interpreted by a trained psychologist – you have a right to ensure that they are professionally administered.
- Staying motivated is hard – everyone goes through a slump sometimes. Find out the motivating techniques that work for you, and use them, no matter how silly they appear to others.

» Try out new closing techniques as much as you can. One thing that distinguishes the top performers from the rest is their enormous repertoire of gambits and angles. Practice role play as much as you can, so your performance during a call improves.

Resources

The present chapter contains a basic guide to some of the key Websites and books to consult when beginning to get to grips with sales and sales management.

SPIN SELLING

The S.P.I.N. Selling Fieldbook: Practical Tools, Methods, Exercises and Resources

Neil Rackham's best-selling book *SPIN Selling* had a profound impact on high-end selling. *The S.P.I.N. Selling Fieldbook* goes a stage further by explaining how to practically apply the method of its forerunner. The first section of the text is basically a reiteration of the SPIN method of selling (focusing on the critical SPIN® questioning behaviors). The author builds on this by demonstrating how to engineer these tools and techniques to individual selling situations with the aid of practical, skill-building exercises in each chapter. In essence, the text addresses the sales of services and capital goods, emphasizing a hands-on implementation of the SPIN method in a wide range of business contexts from localized companies to large multinationals.

A particularly good aspect of this book is the incorporation of real case studies of sales forces at work in prominent international companies at the cutting edge of the sales market (such as Motorola, Johnson & Johnson, and AT&T). Rackham focuses on the various techniques employed by these multinationals to boost sales even with the most difficult customers and clients.

The SPIN method of selling is now being used by half of all Fortune 500 companies to train their sales forces. This book is aimed at the easy implementation of SPIN methods and techniques for companies that have not yet established them. It is also intended to aid companies that are already using the method to reinforce it in teaching sessions and in the field.

Rackham, N. (1996) *The S.P.I.N. Selling Fieldbook: Practical Tools, Methods, Exercises and Resources*, McGraw-Hill, New York.

HIGH-EFFICIENCY SELLING

High-Efficiency Selling: How Superior Salespeople Get That Way

Stephan Schiffman is the author of the highly acclaimed *Cold Calling Techniques* and president of New York-based sales training and consulting company D.E.I. Management Inc., whose clientele include AT&T, Motorola, and U.S. Healthcare. In *High-Efficiency Selling*, he details his successful four-fold sales strategy: prospecting, interviewing, presentation, and closing. In this dynamic text Schiffman claims that the implementation of his novel strategy can reduce the stress of the sales team and promote better sales, enhanced time management, and better long-term business partnerships.

In order to achieve these objectives six criteria are defined: attitude, regarded as the single most important factor in holding onto customers; the creation of a personalized prospecting plan; the executing, refining, and development of the cold call; the so-called "ten commandments" of contacting target companies; the tools, questions, and goals necessary for an effective client interview; and finally, simple – but effective – closing techniques.

Schiffman's attributes of robusticity, guile, and wisdom in the marketplace are conveyed particularly well to the reader in this excellent text. Moreover, the technical scope is particularly broad and on the whole it is written in a stimulating way. This book surely must rank among the best in its subject area and is a prerequisite for the aspiring and established sales technician alike.

Schiffman, S. (1997) *High-Efficiency Selling: How Superior Salespeople Get That Way*, Wiley, New York.

GENERAL SALES AND SALES MANAGEMENT

Sales and Sales Management

The fifth edition of *Sales and Sales Management* by David Jobber and Geoff Lancaster represents an in-depth analysis of the management process from a theoretical and practical perspective. The text is sensibly divided into five sections. The first, Sales Perspective, examines the historical role of selling and assesses its context within marketing. The different categories of buyer are also assessed in order to attempt to gauge how selling may be optimized. The second, Sales Technique, adopts a practical approach, covering sales preparation, the personal selling process, and sales responsibilities. The third, Sales Environment, examines the institutions that sales are conducted through; for instance, industrial, commercial, public, and resale channels. Sales Management, the fourth section, assesses recruitment, selection, motivation and training, and the organization and compensation of sales personnel from a managerial perspective. In the final section, Sales Control, the authors examine budgets and business planning, sales forecasting, and forecasting techniques.

This edition contains a new chapter, "Direct Marketing and Information Technology Application in Sales." This explores the methods of selling that have emerged with technological advances (direct mail, telemarketing, Internet), the impact of technology on the productivity of sales forces, and ways of conducting business. Other additions include a range of cases to enhance effective teaching of sales and sales management, with an emphasis on the practical application of these principles. The text also incorporates a new introduction in the "Sales Settings" chapter, and an expanded discussion of key account management. As in previous editions, the authors continue to focus on the international aspects of selling and sales management in order to reflect the increasing importance of international markets.

Sales and Sales Management is targeted at students studying a range of courses at diploma, undergraduate, and postgraduate levels. It is also an invaluable text for those engaged in the professional sphere of sales and sales management, from salesperson to sales manager.

Jobber, D. and Lancaster, G. (2000) *Sales and Sales Management*, Financial Times/Pearson, Harlow.

THEORY AND PRACTICE OF SALES MANAGEMENT

Sales Management, Theory and Practice

The theory and practice of sales management is one of continual change. In the second edition of *Sales Management, Theory and*

Practice Bill Donaldson skillfully assimilates the key theoretical and practical changes occurring in the industry into the text of this excellent publication. The author focuses on the issues that dictate the responses of organizations to changing markets and competition (for instance, as key account selling, direct marketing, and telesales).

Aspects dealt with include the increasing emphasis on managing sales operations rather than the management of sales personnel. This is manifest in the impact of IT on sales operations (particularly database marketing). The creation and maintenance of relationships between buyers and sellers is also explored with specific regard of how these should be managed. Finally, the text adopts a more international perspective (a parallel trend with most texts in this subject area). This takes into account the recognition for many companies of the necessity to participate in European and global markets.

The second edition incorporates three new chapters (on the sales process; selling in international markets; and ethics in selling and sales management). The remaining chapters have been revised and updated with the addition of three comprehensive case studies. As such this text is a valuable manual for class discussion, training purposes, or academic study.

Donaldson, B. (1997) *Sales Management, Theory and Practice*, Macmillan, Basingstoke.

THE SALES FORCE

Building the High Performance Sales Force

The pressures facing sales managers in the current market have reached an unprecedented level and are manifold. These include the extraction of greater revenues with diminishing support; greater competition within shrinking markets; the consolidation of districts and supervision of larger sales teams; and the incorporation of additional marketing functions. The message conveyed by Joe Petrone in this book is that traditional management approaches to emerging problems are not sufficient; the emphasis instead should be upon adopting new strategies that address the rapidly changing roles and responsibilities of today's overworked sales professionals. These include the implementation of Total Quality Selling; Total Quality Management; and

Progressive Goal Management (PGM), a dynamic that links the targets of sales representatives to corporate performance (and appraises it accordingly).

Another feature of the text is the incorporation of a precise blueprint termed the "120-Day Improvement Plan." This is designed to exemplify the author's high-performance concepts in action, stage by stage. The book is also "humanized" with reference to real-life sales cases and anecdotes. Given the comprehensive scope of this publication and the range of issues dealt with this book will undoubtedly represent a lifeline to the battle-fatigued sales manger of the modern age.

Petrone, J. (1994) *Building the High-Performance Sales Force*, American Management Association, New York.

INTERNET RESOURCES

Government organizations

www.stat-usa.gov

STAT-USA/Internet is the most important source of data on the Internet. STAT-USA, a part of the US Department of Commerce's Economics and Statistics Administration, produces and distributes the most extensive government-sponsored business, economic, and trade information databases in the world today (for a nominal subscription fee), including the National Trade Data Bank, Economic Bulletin Board, and Global Business Procurement Opportunities.

www.census.gov

The Website of the US Census Bureau contains a range of available government data from demographics to economic indications, to keep you informed.

http://govinfo.kerr.orst.edu/index.html

The site of the Government Information Sharing Project containing information on demographics, economics, and education, and a wide scope of events in the United States in general.

Non-government organizations (NGOs)

www.huthwaite.com

Over the past two decades, Huthwaite has gained an international reputation for innovation in sales effectiveness. Most notable was the study that spawned SPIN selling (a program of research that analyzed over 35,000 sales calls, and is considered by many to be the most important study ever conducted in the sales field). The Huthwaite sales library contains a range of information on sales management and SPIN selling including news, books, papers, a newsletter, seminars, and other events.

www.salesandmarketing.com

The Sales and Marketing Management Website provides a comprehensive list of useful sales and marketing Web addresses.

www.dnbmdd.com

The D&B Million Dollar Database provides corporate information on more than 1 million US leading public and private businesses. A range of services are available, from viewing a sample company record to obtaining a free trial database. The user may also search for information by company name, executive name, location, industry, and company size. Company records contain useful corporate information from addresses to sales figures.

www.terralign.com

The TerrAlign Group site provides a useful insight into the design of global sales forces (expatriates, local nationals, and third-country nationals) using US models; in particular, the company has provided tools to help international firms create balanced territories and find optimal locations for sales offices in Canada, Mexico, and Australia.

http://lookupUSA.com

SalesLeadsUSA is a free database service that permits a search for the address and phone number of more than 11 million businesses in the United States and Canada by name, type of business, SIC code, names of key executives, and more.

www.dotcom.com

This site is essentially news and information about the Internet and the economy. The useful search engine locates any type of business with a Web page.

www.mapnp.org

The Free Management Library contains a wealth of information on a range of topics. The sales and marketing sections are particularly good.

http://superpages.GTE.net

The GTE Superpages site has two directory resources for locating any business within the United States. The first contains 5000 yellow-page business directories; the second more than 60,000 business Web addresses that can be searched by keywords or business categories.

www.sell.org

The Sales and Marketing Executives Library is packed with news, statistics, a job search, and many more features.

University-based Websites

www.2000.ogsm.vanderbilt.edu

Based at Vanderbilt University, this site features academic research for electronic marketing.

www.dissertations.org

Networked Digital Library of Theses and Dissertations (NDLTD) enables the user to access a large number of relevant academic papers from this site.

FURTHER READING

Adams, T. (1985) *The Secrets of Successful Selling*, Heinemann, London.
Allen, P. (1993) *Selling: Management and Practice*, 4th edition, M & E Handbooks, Pitman, London.

Anderson, R.E., Hair, J.E., and Bush, A.J. (1992) *Professional Sales Management*, McGraw-Hill, New York.

Barber, M. (1997) *How Champions Sell*, McGraw-Hill, Maidenhead.

Bird, D. (1998) *How to Write Sales Letters that Sell*, Kogan Page, London.

Bolt, G.J. (1987) *Practical Sales Management*, Pitman, London.

Boyatzis, Richard E. (1982) *The Competent Manager: A Model for Effective Performance*, Wiley, New York.

Churchill, G.A. Jr., Ford, N.M., and Walker, O.C. Jr. (1992) *Sales Force Management: Planning, Implementation and Control*, 2nd edition, Irwin, Homewood, Illinois.

Claybaugh, M.G. and Forbes, J.L. (1992) *Professional Selling – A Relationship Approach*, West Publishing, New York.

Coner, J.M. and Dubinsky, A.J. (1985) *Managing the Successful Sales Force*, Lexington Books, Lexington, Massachusetts.

Dalrymple, D.J. (1988) *Sales Management: Concepts and Cases*, Wiley, New York.

Denny, R. (1996) *Selling to Win*, Kogan Page, London.

Elsby, F.H. (1969) *Marketing and Sales Manager*, Pergamon, Oxford.

Fisher, R. and Ury, W. (1989) *Getting to Yes: Negotiating Agreement Without Giving In*, Business Books, London.

Futrell, C.M. (1984) *Fundamentals of Selling*, Irwin, Homewood, Illinois.

Futrell, C.M. (1994) *Sales Management*, Dryden Press, Fort Worth, Texas.

Gabay, J. (1996) *Teach Yourself Copywriting*, Hodder and Stoughton, London.

Gilliam, A. (1982) *The Principles and Practice of Selling*, Heinemann, Oxford.

Hafer, A.C. (1993) *The Professional Selling Process*, West Publishing, St Pauls, Minnesota.

Holmes, G. and Smith, N. (1987) *Salesforce Incentives*, Heinemann, London.

Hunter, J.E. and Hunter, R.F. (1984) "Validity and utility of alternative predictors of job performance," *Psychological Bulletin*, **96**, 72-98.

Jackson, D.W. Jr., Cunningham, W.H., and Cuningham, I.C.B. (1988) *Selling: The Personal Force in Marketing*, Wiley, New York.

Jobber, D. (ed.) (1997) *CIM Handbook of Selling and Sales Strategy*, Butterworth-Heinemann, Oxford.

Kennedy, G., Benson, J., and MacMillan, P. (1980) *Managing Negotiations*, Business Books, London.

Kossen, S. (1982) *Creative Selling Today*, Harper and Row, New York.

Lancaster, G.A., Seekings, D., Wills, G., and Kozubska, J. (1985) *Maximising Industrial Sales*, MCB University Press, Bradford.

Lawrence, J. (1977) *If You're Not Selling, You're Being Outsold*, Wiley, New York.

Leonard, George (1987) "Mastery: Taking it home," *Esquire*, May, 149-52.

Lidstone, J.B.J. (1991) *Manual of Sales Negotiation*, Gower, Aldershot.

Lidstone, J.B.J. (1992) *Beyond the Pay Packet*, McGraw-Hill, New York.

Likert, R. (1961) *New Patterns of Sales Management*, McGraw-Hill, London.

Manchester Open Learning (1998) *Making Effective Presentations*, Kogan Page, London.

Manning, G.L. and Reece, B.L. (1984) *Selling Today: A Personal Approach*, Brown, New York.

March, R.M. (1990) *The Honourable Customer: Marketing and Selling to the Japanese in the 1990s*, Longman Professional, Melbourne.

Mayer, David and Greenberg, Herbert M. (1964) "What makes a good salesman?" *Harvard Business Review*, 119-25.

McDonald Morris (1996) *The Pocket Guide to Selling Services and Products*, Butterworth-Heinemann, Oxford.

Mercer, D. (1988) *The Sales Professional*, Kogan Page, London.

Miller, R.B., Heiman, S.E., and Tuleja, T. (1988) *Strategic Selling*, Kogan Page, London.

Murdock, Alexander and Scutt, Carol N. (1997) *Personal Effectiveness*, Institute of Management Foundation, Butterworth-Heinemann, Oxford.

Nideffer, Robert M. (1976) "Test of Attentional and Interpersonal Style," *Journal of Personality and Social Psychology*, **34**, 394-404.

Nideffer, Robert M. (1987) "Psychological preparation of the highly competitive athlete," *The Physician and Sport Medicine*, **15**, (10), 85-92.

Nideffer, Robert M. and Pratt, Robin W. (1982) "A review of the Test of Attentional and Interpersonal Style," *Enhanced Performance Associates Quarterly Report*, **1**, 1–23.

Noonan, C. (1986) *Sales Management: The Complete Marketer's Guide*, Allen & Unwin, London.

Noonan, C. (1997) *Sales Management*, Butterworth-Heinemann, Oxford.

Oberhaus, M.A., Ratcliffe, S., and Stauble, V. (1993) *Professional Selling: A Relationship Process*, The Dryden Press, Fort Worth, Texas.

Pederson, C.A., Wright, M.D., and Weitz, B.A. (1986) *Selling – Principles and Practice*, 4th edition, Irwin, Homewood, Illinois.

Peters, Tom (1988) *Thriving on Chaos*, Alfred Knopf, New York.

Rackham, N. (1994) *SPIN Selling*, Gower, London.

Rogers, L. (1987) *Handbook of Sales and Marketing Management*, Kogan Page, London.

Schiffman, S. (1997) *25 Top Sales Techniques*, Kogan Page, London.

Seltz, D.D. (1982) *Handbook of Effective Sales Prospecting Techniques*, Addison-Wesley, New York.

Stafford, J. and Grant, C. (1986) *Effective Sales Management*, Butterworth-Heinemann, Oxford.

Stanton, W.J., Buskirk, R.H., and Spiro, R.L. (1991) *Management of the Sales Force*, 8th edition, Irwin, Homewood, Illinois.

Still, R.R., Cundiff, E.W., and Govoni, N.A.P. (1981) *Sales Management: Decisions, Strategies and Cases*, Prentice Hall, New York.

Tack, A. (1989) *Increase Your Sales the Tack Way*, Gower, Aldershot.

Weymes, P. (1990) *Handbook of Sales Management and Training Development*, Kogan Page, London.

Wilson, M.T. (1983) *Managing a Sales Force*, 2nd edition, Gower, Aldershot.

Winkler, J. (1989) *Winning Sales and Marketing Tactics*, Heinemann, London.

Ten Steps to Making Sales Work

» Think outside the box
» Do your own prospecting
» Look for qualifying prospects
» Using Web-based technology
» Selling abroad
» Mastering key account management and relationship selling
» SPIN selling to key accounts
» Staying put as a salesperson
» Master the ''close''
» ''Sell the sizzle, not the steak.''

1. THINK OUTSIDE THE BOX

Products have lifecycles and markets are constantly changing. With their thorough knowledge of their customers, salespeople are in a strong position to judge new products and developing market gaps. Use this knowledge for your benefit – if your firm is resisting change, maybe it is time to look for one that will listen, or enter a faster growing field.

2. DO YOUR OWN PROSPECTING

Although your firm will probably have a system for finding sales prospects, it is wise to generate some of your own. A very effective way of doing this is to regularly exchange leads with salespeople selling non-competing products to a similar type of customer. Regularity is important because you need to trust your colleagues and the quality of the information they give you. Sometimes these schemes can be set up formally, by approaching the sales managers of promising firms.

Another way of finding good prospects is to trawl through the files of salespeople who have left the firm. Frequently there are leads that have fallen through the net, such as a customer who made one purchase two years ago but has not been approached since, or a near-customer who somehow was not "closed." Finding your own quality prospects is a good way of increasing your conversion rate – don't leave it to your firm to decide who you should approach.

3. LOOK FOR QUALIFYING PROSPECTS

A lot of people would like to buy a Porsche but don't have the money or the ability to borrow. In sales jargon, they are not "qualified" prospects. "Qualification" simply means that the customer is likely to need your product and has the means to pay for it.

To prescreen prospects, you need as much information about them as possible. Often this can be obtained by acquaintances who are already satisfied customers, or from exchanging leads and going over old customer records as described above. Keep notes of all your encounters; someone who is not "qualified" now may become so in the future.

4. USING WEB-BASED TECHNOLOGY

Software such as CRM and Sales Force Automation is proving extremely effective in sales support. Customers can often get quicker answers to their queries over matters such as delivery and returns than ever before, either via a Website or through call centres. The information flow between sales support and the sales force has also been improved, and a salesperson can now access the latest details of a customer's activities just before making a call, avoiding the embarrassment of being told "I don't want to buy anything more until your back office people get their act together." For complex sales to large firms, involving many different individuals on both sides, the scope for confusion is great, and Web-based software is helping to ensure that everyone in the sales force is up to speed on developments.

Where CRM and its software relatives are falling down, however, is when they are used to impose a rigid reporting system on salespeople themselves. A busy seller in the field needs to reduce paperwork to a minimum, and being required to input large amounts of data is irksome. Since sales people are often in competition with one another, they also often feel the need to keep certain information to themselves until they have closed a sale and are resisting some of the inputting requirements. Many companies that have installed expensive CRM systems are finding that staff are simply not using them, especially if the original champion of the project leaves the firm.

It's an old story in the IT business. New software promises to solve all problems, but fails to account for the way human beings interact. A top-down approach rarely works; the smart way to introduce new systems is to move gradually and adapt them piecemeal to the company's existing way of working. Once one Web-enabled facility has proved its worth, people will be more willing to contemplate using others.

5. SELLING ABROAD

As trade barriers recede and with developing countries offering the greatest opportunities for sales growth, more and more companies are finding that selling overseas is not an option but a necessity. The problem is that selling abroad is almost always riskier and more expensive. Conditions vary so much between nations that it is rarely possible to enter a market using exactly the same methods that the company employs at home. Usually, local conditions will dictate the approach. Licensing to a local manufacturer is the cheapest way in, but offers the least profit, and in some countries there is a real danger of not being able to protect patents and trademarks. In Russia, for example, there are reports that some major local pharmaceutical companies are secretly making pirated versions of patent medicines while manufacturing the genuine products under license.

Home-country salespeople will usually be involved in only one or two aspects of overseas selling:

» Supporting existing host-country distributors at trade fairs and key local sales calls that require special expertise.
» Dealing with customers from one large multinational as part of "Global Account Management."
» Direct selling high-value or technically complex products and services to a few large overseas customers.

Perhaps the most important thing for a proactive salesperson is to become familiar with the subtle barriers that exist in a foreign market. Local cartels, xenophobia, and political policies do not advertise themselves overtly, and it is often easy to chase apparently promising foreign leads, only to find that insurmountable problems emerge at a later stage. The key is to get to know the country and how your industry operates there. Developing long-lasting relationships is usually essential, so the process takes time. Blitzkrieg-style selling efforts overseas are likely to be unsuccessful.

6. MASTERING KEY ACCOUNT MANAGEMENT AND RELATIONSHIP SELLING

A major trend in sales is toward developing very close ties with a handful of major customers. Although such key accounts may offer a very large sales potential, the supplier needs to protect itself, especially if it is smaller than its major customers. In some industries, giant firms have been known to become so demanding of their key suppliers, particularly in terms of services, that the sellers risk collapse. A healthy relationship can lead to major cost savings and improved joint product development. Salespeople tend to work in teams, feeding back information from different individuals in the customer's firm in order to nurse the sale through to closure. Often, profit margins are pre-agreed, so the salesperson focuses on discussions of quality and efficiency issues rather than price. The difficulty is in getting a final decision. Huthwaite, a prominent sales research organization, recommends focusing on obtaining agreement to action points by the end of each call. For example, a customer may agree to provide access to a more senior person, or to attend a demonstration with colleagues. Salespeople need to find out as much as possible about the company politics and decision processes. Some experts recommend a "stage management" approach, where the salesperson "rehearses" individuals in the customer's organization so that they can champion the product at internal meetings that the salesperson cannot attend.

7. SPIN SELLING TO KEY ACCOUNTS

"SPIN selling" is a proprietary approach developed by the Huthwaite Research Group. The four-part model offers a guideline to the stages in a sales call:

1 Preliminary – establish who you are and why you are here. Obtain the buyer's agreement to ask questions about the business.
2 Investigation – ask the buyer questions to elicit needs. Lead the buyer from "implicit" needs to an "explicit" statement of them, e.g. "What we really need is . . . ."
3 Demonstration – Build up the seriousness of the problem in the customer's mind by discussing the ramifications – for example, how many work hours are lost, how much money is wasted, and so on. Then show the customer that your product can fill the stated need.
4 Commitment – don't try to close, but obtain an agreement on some action point that you can follow up later.

8. STAYING PUT AS A SALESPERSON

For salespeople and employers alike, the very high turnover of sales staff across many industries is a costly and time-consuming problem.

For the individual, the challenge is to find a good company, in the sense of one that offers realistic career paths, is well run, and has good growth prospects. Simply answering an advertisement is not enough – you need to know your industry and discover all you can about the company from others working in the same field. Top sales performers are highly sought after and have little need of recruitment agencies and the like – once you have a great track record, the chances are that potential employers will seek you out.

Psychological tests are expensive and must be professionally administered, so are out of reach of smaller firms. Many large companies use them extensively, however, and there is evidence that they can be effective. Although clever applicants may find ways to "cheat" (try to appear to be something they are not), the most sophisticated tests have ways of weeding these answers out. Like most activities in life, innate aptitude is central to success in sales. Although successful salespeople do not all have the stereotypical pushy extrovert personality, researchers suggest that they do have the ability to "empathize" (put themselves in the customer's shoes) and are "ego-driven" (they get genuine satisfaction from making a sale). As experienced salespeople know, selling isn't easy, and many people who are attracted to the field by dreams of quick money, or see it as a short-term stepping stone to a managerial role, are likely to be disappointed. If you're considering a career in sales, make sure that you really enjoy the process before you start in earnest.

9. MASTER THE "CLOSE"

Closing a sale is the key part of a sales presentation, and top performers generally achieve a much higher conversion rate than the average salesperson. This is partly because top performers have developed skills to filter out "unqualified" prospects and poor leads, but it is also because they are constantly developing and refining their closing techniques. Average salespeople may know of many techniques, but stick to only one or two in a rigid manner, failing to adapt their approach to the customer's personality and circumstances. Great salespeople often have an uncanny ability to assess situations, and have a large repertoire of memorized tactics they can call upon. Customer objections are often predictable, and salespeople who know their product well spend time rehearsing ways of overcoming them. There are many ways to counteract refusals on grounds of cost, for example, assuming that you know that the customer can actually afford to pay. In general, customers, particularly business customers, do not mind dealing with a highly motivated salesperson, since they are likely to get accurate answers and an efficient service. What nobody wants is a seller with dog-eared brochures, poor presentation skills, and no ability to listen to the customer's needs.

The "close" is often difficult because customers dislike being put on the spot. One of the arts of successful closing is to manage the conversation so that the presentation merges imperceptibly into the order without the buyer noticing a change in atmosphere; for instance, some sellers ruin the "close" by suddenly becoming tense, or changing their tone of voice. One effective method to nurture a smooth transition is to use the order form as a way of taking notes about the customer's needs. If the customer reminds you that he or she has not yet made a decision, you agree at once but say that you don't want to waste their time by fussing over details later.

10. "SELL THE SIZZLE, NOT THE STEAK"

This old saying remains perennially true. By associating your product with things that people always want, such as youth, beauty, happiness, power, and so on, the object becomes much more than its components. Most consumers are perfectly well aware of this phenomenon, sometimes known as "magical thinking," yet they are still affected by its seduction. What is your product's "sizzle?"

KEY LEARNING POINTS

» Do your own prospecting to increase your sales.
» Develop your ability to identify "qualified" prospects – exchange leads with salespeople in non-competing firms and trawl old customer files.
» If you're interested in foreign sales, get to know individual countries well – every foreign market is different, despite appearances.

- Key account management requires a constant flow of information about the customer. If the key account is too large, sales may become transactional, and unprofitable. Middle-sized customers may produce better results.
- Many salespeople do not stay long in a firm, which is unsatisfactory for both them and their companies. Research your firm thoroughly before applying to work there, and make sure that it is right for you.
- "Closing" is an art form that you can constantly improve upon. The best closers are highly sought after – become one of them if you can.

Frequently Asked Questions (FAQs)

Q1: What is CRM?

A: See Chapter 4, throughout.

Q2: When is licensing the best way to sell abroad?

A: See Chapter 5, Licensing.

Q3: Why do great new products often have a tough time getting introduced?

A: See Chapter 5, Best practice: Dyson.

Q4: What is "Global Account Management?"

A: See Chapter 6, Global account management (GAM) in the PC industry.

Q5: What is SPIN selling?

A: See Chapter 6, SPIN selling.

Q6: What is "open accounting?"

A: See Chapter 6, Relationship selling and the "Quality" movement.

Q7: When did branding start?

A: See Chapter 3, The nineteenth century.

Q8: What is Maslow's hierarchy of needs?

A: See Chapter 3, Maslow's hierarchy of needs.

Q9: What have TQM and JIT to do with sales?

A: See Chapter 6, Relationship selling and the "Quality" movement.

Q10: What is a "trial close?"

A: See Chapter 2, "Closing".

Index

EXPRESSEXEC –
BUSINESS THINKING AT YOUR FINGERTIPS

ExpressExec is a 12-module resource with 10 titles in each module. Combined they form a complete resource of current business practice. Each title enables the reader to quickly understand the key concepts and models driving management thinking today.

Available from:
www.expressexec.com

Customer Service Department
John Wiley & Sons Ltd
Southern Cross Trading Estate
1 Oldlands Way, Bognor Regis
West Sussex, PO22 9SA
Tel: +44(0)1243 843 294
Fax: +44(0)1243 843 303
Email: cs-books@wiley.co.uk

Printed in the United States
By Bookmasters